TITLE:

The Estrangement of Black Male Youth:
From a Teacher's Perspective

Author: Jerald McNair

Copyright Year: 2005
Copyright Notice: by Jerald McNair. All rights reserved

Results in this copyright notice:

© 2005 by Jerald McNair. All rights reserved.

No part of this book may be reproduced or transmitted in any form or by any means without the expressed written consent of the publisher.

ISBN: 1-4116-6262-8

Preface

How do we get our black male youth to do better? So many are going in and out of jail; so many are dropping out of school; so many are in school, but failing miserably. What can be done now to put the brakes on what is happening in America, where we have black male youth going one way and white males going in another direction?

Many of the solutions are not going to come from outside of our community. We can't continue to blame society for some of the things we can change on our own. Many of the solutions have to come from within our own communities. We should be tired of black male youth killing each other, not taking school seriously, and making residents feel vulnerable in their own communities.

As a black male educator, I've seen black male youth at their best and at their worst. I know they can do better. With the proper changes and solutions we can get them of the streets, out of the gangs, and away from selling drugs.

In this book, I first detail what I believe to be some of the problems, as to why many black male youth are doing the aforementioned. I then focus on some of the changes and solutions to the problems. I truly believe we, as black people, are in a critical point in our history. We must make major changes in how we are raising our males, and teaching them, if our communities are going to improve. We can't continue to turn a blinds eye to what is going on. We are loosing too many of our youth to jail and early graves.

The basic theme of this book focuses on what black fathers can do to improve the lives of their sons, their homes, and their communities. I'm challenging every black male, particularly the fathers, to do better. We must!

ACKNOWLEDGMENTS

I would like to dedicate this work to my parents, Margo and Charles McNair, my wife and son, Denise and Andre. Because this book is mostly about fatherhood, I would like to especially thank my father. He was always there for his family, during the good times and tough times. No matter how difficult things might have been on occasion, he never wavered in his support. I also appreciate the guidance I receive from my brother, as he works diligently to maintain a good relationship with his children.

I also would like to acknowledge some men I view as role models because of their strong commitment to raising their sons and daughters the "right" way: Charles Thomas, Billy Flennoy, Lawrence Taylor, Jermaine Flennoy, Kelvin Smith, James Rodgers, Gregory Wright, Donald Davenport, Kurt Jackson,

Eddie Caffey, Mr. Jones, Lorenzo Davis, Uncle Barn, Cornell Stamply, Walt Smith, Buddy Beverly, Jimmy Warren and, indeed, Charles Greggory Thomas, and once again my father and brother respectively, Charles McNair and Charles Andre McNair.

I've observed all of you at one time or another exhibit patience, understanding, and love towards your children. You all epitomize the essence of being good fathers. The commitment you all have shown inspired me greatly, as I wrote this book. I thank you.

Contents

Title   i
Preface   ii
Acknowledgements   v
Contents   vii
Introduction   1

Chapter I: Black Males and Their Sons   8
   Blame Game   10
   The Black Community   13
   What Is Going On In The Home?   16
   Why Some Black Men May Not Feel Responsible For Their Plight   21
   Criticism-Is It True?   27
   Music   30
   Conversations During Dinner   36
   Video Games   43
   Good Citizenship   45
   Parents Practice Good Citizenship   49
   Voting   51
   Reading   55
   Promptness   59
   Career Choices   62

Chapter II: Decreasing the Achievement Gap   67
   Hiring Practices   75
   Educational Forums   79
   Vocational/Cooperative Schools   81

Residential Public Schools   87
Chapter III: Ways to Educate Black Males   91
Chapter IV: The Purpose of This Book   107
Chapter V: A Teacher's Challenge   111
Chapter VI: The Challenge for Black Men   115
Chapter VII: What Can Black Women Do To Improve The Relationship Between Fathers and Sons?   120
Chapter VIII: The Conclusion   126
Notes: 136

Introduction

I am an African American male educator. I've been teaching for about nine years. When I was deciding on choosing a career, I limited myself to two choices: becoming a lawyer or an educator. I was tempted to choose the former because of two reasons: the enormous potential to make a lot of money and the prestige that goes with being a lawyer. On average lawyers generally make more than those in other occupations outside of medicine. Moreover, the prestige that comes with the job is significant. People generally view them as being highly intelligent, sophisticated, ambitious and wealthy.

When I was deciding on careers, those factors weighed heavily in my decision. After graduating with a Bachelors Degree, I thought long and hard about law school. During this time, I started working at an alternative school as a part-time non-certified teacher. During my stay there, I worked with students that had been removed from regular school settings because of problems, ranging from fighting students to attacking teachers. The vast majority of them were African American males.

Unfortunately, most of them were not interested in getting an education. They had to attend because they were kicked out of the regular school, and some had legal issues; therefore, they had to portray themselves in a positive light for the judge, or they attended because they were going to be kicked out of the house if they didn't. Based on this, it's is quite obvious that education was not their primary reason for being in school.

As I worked with this population, I learned a lot about life and the school system. In terms of the former, I learned that if you make "bad" decisions in life at an early age it will negatively affect your life forever. I learned that life for many black male students is significantly different than those of others. The former is more likely to be frustrated, rebellious, unsuccessful in school, and apathetic to the whole educational process.

Furthermore, I learned that many schools, in their present form, are ill equipped to meet and address the needs of these students, and not because they don't care to, but because the needs of these students are quite different from what is offered in many schools across America.

These thoughts began to develop after about four months of working in the alternative setting. From the time I started teaching, and up to the present, I still believe far too many black males are not interested in the educational system because it doesn't meet their needs. The question that begs for consideration is: What are their needs? While I'll address those needs later; I will say that most of these needs center around developing the whole person (i.e. social, physical and mental areas) rather than focusing solely on academics. It's this premise that gave me the impetus to write this book. Teaching and observing these students on a daily basis gives me a tremendous amount of insight as to why so many black male students are so unsuccessful in our public school system. The lack of fathers in the home, the view that getting an education is for "chumps," the negative influences in the community, and an unstable home life contribute substantially to the failed efforts and indifference so many black male students exhibit in school.

Because many black youth grow up in fatherless homes, they don't see black males on a daily basis that maybe doing positive things, such as going to work, reading, and raising a family. Quite conversely, they see women (i.e. their mother, aunt, cousin) doing positive things stated above. This sends a message that getting an education or working everyday is reserved only for women. And for men that may do it, they are viewed as aberrations or perhaps "chumps," or even "wimps." These men can be easily dismissed because they represent something that is so different, than what these youth are used to seeing.

In chapter 1, I elaborate more on this. In particular, I focus on the mind set I see black male youth exhibit on a daily basis, a mind set which devalues education. I'll also address fourteen factors that I've seen reflected in the behavior and attitude of many of the black male youth I taught, and many of those taught by my colleagues, that are influencing them either directly or indirectly in a way that is hindering them from being able to succeed in education: (1) blaming society rather than themselves for some things they can change; (2) bad influences in the black community; (3) the negative influences in the home; (4) the lack of responsibility felt by black men, which results in a poor relation between them and their sons (5) the uneasiness we have with criticizing each other when it's necessary; (6) some of the music we allow into our home that have destructive lyrics; (7) conversations we have during dinner time that are harmful; (8) video games we allow children to play with that may be harmful; (9) our failure to talk about the importance of "good citizenship;" (10) the failure on the part of parents to practice "good citizenship;" paying bills; (11) the tendency we have to not vote, which impacts the quality of the services we get in our community; (12) the harmful of affects of not modeling reading to our children; (13) promptness and the idea that blacks operate under a different system affectionately known as "cp time;" (14) focusing on the importance of talking about career choices in the lives of black youth, and the consequences that occur when we don't. In chapter II, I'll then focus on solutions to decreasing the achievement gap of black youth, particularly black boys, relative to others. In chapter III, I discuss how black young males should be educated. The steps and strategies I use to motivate them are analyzed. I then reflect on the impetus, and the indirect influences, behind me writing this book. The next part focuses on a challenge I propose to black men to do a better job raising their sons, being more productive in their communities, and changing some poor behaviors that are negatively affecting their families, particularly their relationships with black male youth. I then encourage black women to support the relationship between fathers and their sons. I then end with a conclusion.

Chapter I

Black Males and Their Sons

Black males must do a better job raising their sons. That means black fathers must not only stay in the lives of their sons, but should build a quality relationship with them, one that is based on trust, commitment and love. It's essential that black boys trust that their fathers are going to be there as they grow up. For far too long, the black community has accepted the fact that too many black men have not lived up to their responsibility. Far too many black boys feel that sooner or later their fathers will desert them. This belief as been buttressed by what they see in their communities: single-family homes, headed up by women, mothers struggling financially to raise their families without a male adult in the home. This insecure feeling promotes self-doubt and negatively impacts their self-esteem. This poor self-image is portrayed when black boys matriculate through the school system. They are more likely to end up in special education, more likely to get suspended or expelled from school, and more likely to underachieve. Once they develop a pattern of not achieving in school, or getting in trouble, it's hard to break it. They begin to expect to do poorly, and everyone associated with them begin to expect it as well.

It is essential that black fathers establish a relationship with their sons because it gives them confidence and the assurance that their fathers will always be there for them, and will help to curb some of the negative things that are affecting so many black boys besides that listed above: dropping out of school, not working, selling drugs, and going to prison.

The Blame Game

Racism is an evil sickness that causes society and those that are victims of it a great deal of pain. Racism is the belief that other races are inferior and therefore must be treated differently. It is an unfortunate sickness that continues to exist. Unfortunately, black men encounter it daily, be it in the grocery store when shopping for goods, or in a clothing store, when we're followed by security, be it standing in an elevator with a white individual that appears uncomfortable and starts holding their possessions tighter, or be it by the hands of a police officer that stops black motorists because they are driving a nice car in a non-black neighborhood. Indeed, racism is alive and well.

Unfortunately, the power of it seems to have discouraged many black men. They seem defeated in many cases, and lack the drive and motivation to do what is necessary to be successful in America. An example of this happened to me while I was teaching in Chicago. One day after school I was talking to one of my male students about the importance of getting an education and staying in school. While I was talking to him, his eyes started watering. He was getting emotional because he was witnessing his father, who was down the street, digging in the garbage can for food. Here I was talking about school, while this young man was watching his father eat out of the garbage can. Any man that would allow his son to see that in the mist of his friends has given up hope, and is full of despair.

In the school where I use to teach, about three miles down the road, I would pass a liquor store around 7:30 am every morning. Almost everyday, I would see a group of black men standing in front of the store waiting to purchase liquor. I was tempted to go over there and lecture them not only about the value of working, but how bad it looks, and the message it is sending to kids as they go off to school. Unfortunately, this example occurs all too often in many black communities early in the morning on a daily basis. Many black men have simply given up hope of ever working a regular job, of ever raising a family, or of ever being responsible.

For years or even decades, it's been acceptable to argue that racism has been the cause of many of the negative things that impact blacks. High unemployment, substandard education, poverty, teenage pregnancy and crime filled neighborhoods etc… have been in one form or another linked to racism.

To the extent that there is a cause and effect relationship between racism and the social ills that continue to have a deleterious affect on blacks, have in my opinion made some black men feel that they are not responsible for what goes on in their communities, their homes, and even in their own lives. This sense of not feeling responsible has been extremely damaging to what is going on in our black communities, in our homes, and in the lives of so many black men. They are more likely to be unemployed than white males, more likely to dropout of high school compared to whites, and as I see on a daily basis as a teacher more likely to be uninterested in school as they grow up.

The Black Community

I will not spend much time talking about what is going on in the black community that negatively impacts young black males. However, in order to strengthen my argument, it must be addressed.

The businesses and the institutions in the black community contribute mightily to the dysfunctional behavior of our black youth. Take for example the liquor stores. As mentioned above, in many black communities, you will see dozens of black men standing in front of liquor stores early in the morning. While this is happening, young black boys are going to school, witnessing this daily. This sends a direct message to them. First, they begin to accept the stereotype that black men are lazy and don't desire to work. It also trivializes education by suggesting that it's something you seek early in life only because the law requires you to go to school, not because you will need it later in life. These messages are adhered to early in the lives of young black boys. Therefore, it is not surprising that many black boys are no longer interested in school at an early age. It's been my experience that the educational gap, between black and white boys, start at an early age, a gap that widens as they both matriculate through the school system.

In my experience as a teacher, it is extremely challenging to motivate far too many black boys to take school seriously, when they reach the intermediate grade level. At the primary level, which is kindergarten to third grade, they are filled with so much enthusiasm and energy to learn. However, as they matriculate through school, they begin to become more cognizant of their surroundings. They see many black men not working, or not going to school. They see many black teenagers hanging on the street corners, dropping out of school, and in some cases selling drugs. All of these negative things are converging on these black boys, and it affects their psyche. They begin to become disruptive and rebellious in school because they don't see the connection between school and what they believe they will be doing later in life. I compare it to someone who is at a place that he doesn't want to be. In order to get out, the individual fights and causes disruptions to bring attention to himself, in an effort to get removed.

It has been my experience that if you examine the number of detentions, suspensions, and expulsions that are given out, black boys typically receive the majority of them in predominantly black schools and white schools that have some blacks that attend. When they get these admonitions, they are sending a message that school isn't for them, and that they don't want to be there.

Many people have argued that it's the school system that has let these youth down, that schools don't do enough to help these at-risk students. To some extent that is true. Schools have to be more creative in teaching black boys, more innovative in their approaches. At the same, however, I believe a major contributor to the problem is what is going on outside of the school walls. What is in that community and in that home that they see and hear on a daily basis impacts them the most.

I do believe the schools must do a better job at meeting these youth where they are; however, the black community must begin to accept the fact that our communities have contributed mightily perhaps unintentionally to the negative and disruptive behavior of our youth. Steps have to be taken to stop this.

What Is Going On In The Home?

The home life of blacks is filled with many complexities. The black men have a higher rate of unemployment than other men; black teens are more likely to be high school dropouts. The homes are more likely to be single-headed households headed up by women. There is also a higher rate of teenage pregnancy, and a higher probability of having a male sibling in jail. If only one of these situations exist in the home, certainly there would probably be more arguments in the home, a higher level of tension and strife. If two of these situations exist, there would be even more tension and strife in the home. Before I continue, let me state that I'm not suggesting that these situations are limited to black households. Certainly many families, notwithstanding their race, have at least one or perhaps even more of these situations in their households. I'm simply stating that there is a higher percentage of these situations existing in black households.

The by-product of some of these situations is the negative impact it has on children, particularly black boys. After all, boys are taught that when they become adults they are to be the breadwinners in the family, the leader in the family, and indeed the strong one. Therefore, as they grow up and witness a great deal of strife and dissonance in the family, they are more likely to feel angry and upset, and therefore respond more negatively.

This has a devastating affect on the mental state of black boys. On a daily basis I witness them coming to school filled with so much rage and frustration, getting involved in arguments at the start of school, lashing out at teachers, administrators, and their peers without warning. Often times, I would talk to some of my students, particularly the males, about what happened at home or around the neighborhood before I started with my lesson. If I didn't acknowledge their frustration about something that occurred outside of school, I wouldn't get full participation. In other words, they would be preoccupied, or take their frustration out on the class by being disruptive or uncooperative. And, even if they weren't being disruptive, they wouldn't be fully listening to the instructions and the lesson, therefore learning very little.

I had to be aware of what was going on in their household on a weekly basis in order to properly teach them. To abreast myself of what was going on in their homes, I made routine home visits. Almost every Saturday, I made three or four home visits in the morning. Even in areas that were crime filled, I still had to go. Just like I had to equip myself with the book knowledge in order to successfully teach them, I also had to equip myself with the knowledge of what their home life was like. Who had the greatest impact on their lives in the home, be it positive or negative? Who worked and didn't work? How many siblings lived in the house? Did other relatives live in the house? Who was raising them? Did they have to baby sit after leaving school? Where did they go after school? And, what was their relationship with their parents like? It usually was only one parent unfortunately.

If I was going to be successful in teaching them, I had to know these things. When a problem came about, I would have some idea as to who to contact beside the parent, what question to ask, and some idea as to what the root of the problem was. That doesn't mean I was always successful utilizing this method; however, it did allow me to deescalate some situations and prevent some from happening. Furthermore, it made the relationship stronger that I had with my students, particularly the more challenging ones. I learned early in my career as a teacher that if I could find out what was going in my students' households it would have an enormous impact on how well my lessons went. I can use the most effective teaching methods, the latest technology strategies, and be the most energetic and enthusiastic teacher ever, it won't matter much if I'm not able to effectively communicate with my students. When I say communicate, I mean more than give directions and instructions for a lesson, more than respond to a question they may have, I mean understand how they are feeling inside about who they are as people, understand what has or is happening in their home that might have made them angry, understand why they're having mood swings, or having a hard time keeping awake in class. That's what I mean my communication.

Indeed, I was only able to do this by visiting their homes, seeing who was there, on a daily basis, and seeing my students interact with their family members. This equipped me with the knowledge I needed to effectively teach them.

Many of their households were not idea. Some parents had never worked a regular job. Some of the homes were not that cleaned. Simply put, some had deplorable conditions. Unfortunately, I almost never saw fathers in the home. Often times the mothers had a dual role: Serving as mother and father. This was difficult for them and sometimes overwhelming. Many mothers told me that they had never worked and was finally looking for a job, or that the fact they were now looking for work meant they couldn't come up to the school to check on their children. One parent even told me that going to work for the first time in her child's life angered her son, because that meant she was not able to be there whenever he needed her.

It was during many of my discussions that I began to come up with many solutions myself. The parents were either too busy getting their life together or too busy with younger children to devote a great deal of time and energy to the older ones. I further realized that even though I needed to know what was going on in the child's home, I couldn't always depend on the parents for help. I had to be a lot more observant and persistent in order to get the information I needed.

Why Some Black Men May Not Feel Responsible For Their Plight

I believe that the difficult struggles black men face on a daily basis has to some extent taken away the drive and determination of some of them. As alluded to above because racism is still prevalent it seems like many black men have given up hope of being able to hold down a steady job and raise a family, particularly those that didn't have a father in the home when they were growing up. They are blaming racism on their plight; therefore, absolving themselves of all responsibility concerning raising their children, and taking care of their families. The rationalization goes like this: "The white man doesn't want to hire me. When I go to fill out an application, they probably throw it out anyway. If I do get a job, it won't pay much money; so, why should I? For get all this stuff about working, I'll get buy. I'll get me a hustle." Unfortunately, that hustle often time means selling drugs. It's no secret that many black men are in prison for drug related offenses. The young teenagers see so many men going to jail because of drugs that they become desensitized to the fact that once you get caught it will exact a tremendous burden on you and your family.

Unfortunately, this almost inevitable consequence does not serve as a disincentive. While working as teacher in an inner city school, I was certain some of my male students were selling drugs. Often times they would have a substantial amount of cash on them. I would also over hear some of them talk about what they did on the street to get the cash. Even though they would talk around, I was able to pick up on some of the dialogue. I remember one day in particular, I was bold enough to ask a student, "Where did you get the money?" He laughed it off and walked away. The next day he said to me, "I bet you I got more money in my pocket than you have in yours." I was certain he was correct. After all, I knew quite well how little I had in my pocket. I was so shocked that I forgot that I was the one who brought up the conversation, in an effort to guide him in the right direction. I replied, "We are not here to talk about that stuff. We are here for an education." He replied, "Yea you're educated, but broke." I looked at him in amazement because he was attempting to get me to persuade him to stop selling drugs. I accepted this challenge and went on to inform him that drugs dealers often times end up in prison or dead, and that the cost of selling drugs, which is the possibility of death, far outweigh the benefits. I discussed with him that education gives you options and opens up doors. It allows you to wake up every morning not worrying about someone shooting you.

The student was quite surprised that I was willing to talk in length about this subject. Put another way, he was surprised that I was being open and honest about the drug culture and the negative consequences it has had on others. After all, these are generally not topics that are talked about in school, particularly at the middle school level.

The unfortunate thing is it should be. Simply put, many teenagers and pre-teens are selling drugs, and using them. It is no secret that scores of youth, particularly black teenage males are overrepresented in our penal institutions because they are selling drugs. To the extent that many of them don't have positive male role models that are educating them on the dangers of selling drugs, they need to be educated formally in school. Unfortunately, many of them are not.

Well, as the conversation between he and I came to an end, he appeared to be thankful that I shared my feelings with him regarding the topic. He kept looking me straight in the eyes, as I was talking, and he would occasionally shake his head indicating he agreed with me. The last thing I told him was, "Drugs will get you killed." Unfortunately, we never talked about this subject again.

As I was driving home that day, I thought about the impact this conversation had on me, and the tremendous task I had in front of me of trying to convince this young man, my student, to stay clear of drugs. The strange thing is that the circumstances and the opportunity that gave rise to this conversation never came up again. It seemed as if the time was never right to talk about this subject again. As I reflect on it now, I think perhaps it did, in an indirect way, and I just simply tried to avoid it. Perhaps I didn't think I was equipped to advise this young man about something that was so destructive as drugs. Perhaps I was overwhelmed. I'm not sure. I do know that the student and no other student sought my advice again about the topic, and I think I let them down. I should've been more able and better prepared to talk about this issue, rather than simply state that, "It can kill you." Even with the home visits I did and the amount of time I spent trying to form a relationship with the parents and guardians of my students, I was not able to meet the needs of my students in that area. This was quite frustrating to me.

I think many teachers share my same dilemma. Often times, we want to discuss subjects that are not germane to the core subject areas, but are essential, nonetheless, to the lives of our students. However, we have a curriculum in school that we must follow, one that we are held accountable for teaching. As a result, many teachers try to avoid it or talk around a topic that may be tough to deal with, or may be questionable.

Teaching in the inner city means that there are going to be many occasions where teachers will feel the need to share information that will improve the health and the well being of their students. Consequently, they'll have to make tough choices between saying or suggesting something that will help their students and saying something that may get them in trouble. Unfortunately, I was not equipped to help that young man find the answers he needed. If I could do it all over again, I would tell him that there is more to life than selling drugs. Unfortunately, so many of them think that it isn't and the lack of black male role models in their communities support their belief that the lives of black men young or old are quite different from the lives of others. So different that, the traditional way of living such as working a 9 to 5 to job, raising a family etc… are not only unattainable, but not expected for black males.

 This ideology supports the belief that black men should not be held responsible for the things they do because the white man left them no choice. This type of reasoning must stop if we are going to ameliorate the conditions of blacks in America.

Black young men must be told in schools, at home, at church etc… over and over that selling drugs, not working, not going to school, not valuing education, and having babies without taking care of them is not acceptable.

In short, I must make clear that blacks can no longer tolerate this type of behavior because it is counterproductive. As a black male teacher, I make it my responsibility to spend extra time advising my students, particularly my black male students about life. I no longer make the mistake I made years ago that I mentioned above. I have more confidence in dealing with this topic, and I'm willing to risk being reprimanded by administration when I cross over that line, in an effort to possibly save the life of one of my students. I, indeed, welcome the challenge and the opportunity to try to in still values and a sense of purpose to my students. I challenge others, particularly black men to do the same. The time is now. These young men need guidance and direction. We can't pass this responsibility on to others. It's our duty to help these young men reach their full potential.

Criticism—Is It True?

It is difficult being black and being critical of black people. The history of blacks is filled with pain and suffering. Slavery, segregation, lynching, institutional racism, and discrimination are all things black have been subjected to. Still today the playing field is not leveled. Blacks still are more likely to end up in poverty, attend poor performing schools, drop out of high school, and serve time in a penal institution.

I communicate to my students that the poor choices and bad decisions they make can have a deleterious affect on their lives. I do criticize bad decisions that they make, while challenging them to do better. In May of 2004 at a special event in Washington Constitutional Hall, Dr. Bill Cosby was being honored. It was an event that commemorated the 50th Anniversary of Brown v. Board of Education. Dr. Cosby was highly criticized for finding fault with how blacks raise their children. He stated that, "Many blacks would rather buy expensive gym shoes rather than spend their money on books that would educate them" (Chicago Tribune, May 23, 2004). Dr. Cosby was criticized by some black people for saying something which many thought shouldn't have been said in the presence of whites. According to some, something of this magnitude should be kept in house. In other words, it should've only been said in front of blacks.

Traditionally, blacks have not been cool to the idea of publicly criticizing each other in the presence of whites. We often think that in some sense we are letting them-meaning whites-off the hook, not holding them accountable for the racism and discrimination we have been subjected to.

On the other hand, some blacks not only agreed with Dr. Bill Cosby but they welcomed the public criticism. They maintain that the victimization role that we so readily assume doesn't ameliorate our plight. But, in a sense, works against us by alienating other races because it presents itself as a them against us attitude, therefore only promoting a negative response from whites, one that is intolerant and unsympathetic to the plight of blacks, and one that fails to recognize that racism and discrimination still exist.

Bill Cosby's criticism is the same type of speech I routinely give my students, particularly my black males. I tell them to, practice self-discipline. Be responsible for your own behavior. Don't blame others for your failure. Everyday is a new day. What are you going to do to make your life better for yourself today? Excuses for not doing your homework, not listening in class, and not giving 100% are not acceptable. I say things like this repeatedly in order for them to take ownership of their successes and failures.

I believe, as well as Dr. Bill Cosby, that constructive criticism is not only acceptable but is also wise. To not challenge children and parents to do better, and curtail self-destructive behavior, is sending the wrong message, particularly to the former. They are the most impressionable. If we don't speak out in a constructive way against the type of behavior that is destroying the lives of so many youth and so many communities, we would be remiss in our duties.

Blacks must begin to analyze their own behavior and work to change those things that continue to negatively impact our communities. Selling drugs, allowing so many liquor stores in our communities, quitting school, and not taking school seriously are things we can work to improve. Seeing the harmful affects of these, on a daily basis, in the eyes of my students is frustrating. We can and we must do better.

Let me end by saying, our self-image, as blacks, should not be so fragile that we can't accept criticism, particularly criticism that is justifiable. We must limit and change our behavior that is hurting our communities, and hurting our kids.

Music

The music we listen to can influence the things we do, and how we feel as adults. Feelings of depression, loneliness, and sadness are often improved or made worse by listening to music. When we get in to the car, and we turn the radio on, often times it inspires us. We begin to sing along with the song in a jovial way. Indeed, the impact of music on our state of mind is enormous. Unfortunately, some of the music that our black youth are being exposed to is negatively affecting their mind and their sense of who they are. Certain music, particularly that which supports violence, promotes destructive behavior, such as selling drugs, disrespecting women in the form of name calling (i.e. "bitch," "hoe," "and hood rat") should not be listened to by young impressionable youth. Parents should not buy this type of music, nor should they allow their children to. Indeed, parents must be the grown-ups. Stating unequivocally that music like this is not allowed into the house also sends a message to children that it is not acceptable to behave in this manner. Children sometimes have difficulty differentiating between what's real and what's fantasy. If they are allowed to listen to destructive lyrics, at a relatively young age, it will affect how they act.

I'm in no way suggesting that all rap music is bad. That couldn't be further from the truth. Some of it has excellent lyrics and is quality music. However, some of it promotes negative behavior and poor attitudes in our children by glorifying selling drugs, and finding a short cut to success. When youth routinely listen to this, sooner or later, it impacts how they view the world and their place in it. The feeling that the only way to be successful in life is to find an illegal hustle is the result of being imbued with this type of thinking. It's human nature to want to find an easy way to gain wealth. However, when that way features selling drugs, gang banging, and pimping, that must be denounced.

Many of the music videos should also be censored by parents. Once again, I'm not suggesting that all or even most are unfavorable. I'm referring to those that feature fancy cars, women, and the "bling, bling," (gold chains etc.) while talking about hustling illegally in order to acquire wealth. Often times, the message is indirect, and not easily noticeable. However, children know what the message is, both the indirect and the direct message.

While artist have every right to say what they like because it's their constitutional right, parents also have an obligation to protect their children from things that are harmful.

As a teacher, I witness students referencing musical lyrics on a daily basis. If it has a negative connotation that puts down women or glorifies street hustling, I quickly correct the student. I'll say things such as, "That's inappropriate." Or, "Pick another song to sing because that's degrading." I almost never pretend that it's okay to recite lyrics that are destructive. Keep in mind that I'm not referring to swearing words only. After all, we can all agree that children should never be allowed to say those types of words. I'm referring to lyrics that have an implied and an indirect message that promote violence and self-destructive behavior. Say for example a student says, "Hustling is the name of the game, and I do what it takes to gain fame." My response would be, "Education should be your claim to fame because fame doesn't come easily."

The reason behind these responses is to let my students know what is right and what is wrong. Often times, they may not be able to tell the difference because they see negative images promoting violence and drugs in their homes, in their communities, on television, and on the radio.

Often times my students laugh it off and reply that they don't condone the life style, but that they are only singing or rapping about a song. My response is normally, "Perhaps you don't condone the life style; however, it's my job to let you know what represents good and what represents bad."

The exchange between the student and I is not a shouting match or a situation, where I'm belittling or putting the student down. That approach would only result in a negative reply and cause the student to get defensive and argumentative. It's done in a non-threatening way. Nevertheless, my point gets across.

If all adults that students come in contact with supported this philosophy, we could begin to change the destructive behavior that seems to have taken hold over so many of our children today. When I talk to parents at home or at school, I often ask, "How is your child doing at home?" Is he behaving well? I do this to send a message that I am concern about their child not only at school, but also at home. I'm further illustrating that the job of parenting and teaching are twenty-four hour jobs, and that we are all in this together. When parents and teachers discover this and begin sending the same message to children, they respond in a positive way. Positive behavior begins to replace negative behavior. They begin to share the values that we are working so diligently to in still. Those values include having a high regard for education, doing your homework daily, coming to school prepared to learn, getting to bed on time, and understanding that the decisions you make now will impact your life in the near future.

I have conversations with parents regarding their child's hobbies, their friends, and the type of music they listen to, in an effort to let the parents know that all these things matter in the development and growth of children. The influences are many. Television, friends, video games, music, and family members all influence the child's behavior. My home visits communicate to my students that I expect good behavior in school as well as at home.

Fortunately, many parents respond positively when they realize how much I care and what length I'll go to in order to educate their children—my students. I believe it starts first with changing their attitude and then their behavior soon follows. Indeed, negative influences that feature education as being inconsequential must be counteracted and rebuffed. These destructive influences are impacting black youth, particularly males in a negative way. I don't need to quote statistics to show that so many black youth are hustling illegally, and therefore ending up in jail. It is well documented that many are engaging in behavior that has resulted in them being killed and housed in prison disproportionately.

Something has to be done to put an end to this. Before these youth become men, lets change their behavior, their lamented look on life, their view that education is not for them, but for others, their view that education is for "chumps," their view that having kids by different women makes them a man, their view that the white man is not going to allow them to succeed, their view that the way to make it in the world is to hustle illegally, and their view that it is okay to not work at legitimate jobs because they pay minimum wage. If we can change their mind set, we can change what they do.

When I'm in the classroom teaching, I'm concerned not only with teaching the core subjects, but with teaching youth that their attitude may need to be adjusted in order for them to be successful. When I'm successful at changing their approach to education, it normally follows that they do well. Indeed, they have the ability. It's just a matter of getting them to realize that being smart is okay, getting good grades is okay and embracing learning is okay.

Conversations During Dinner

After a hard days work, often times, parents come home talking about how the day went over the dinner table. More times than not, we tend to complain about co-workers, bosses, and the overall climate of the workplace. If our boss happens to be white, we often mention that during the course of the conversation. If we are having trouble at work, such as feeling mistreated, underutilized, or devalued, we bring race into the equation. We may say things such as, "I'm so tired of that racist boss." "Those white folks at work are working my last nerve." Or, "That whole company is racist." These statements may indeed be true. There are many blacks experiencing difficulty at the workplace because of the color of their skin. The problem is that these conversations are being had in front of children. They hear how their parents are frustrated with their jobs and how white people are viewed as the main reason why. These conversations send a message to children to dislike white people, and to be suspicious of all things that represent authority (i.e. bosses, teachers, and administrators).

Children begin to identify with their parents and adopt their philosophy that the "system" is out to get blacks, the system meaning schools, the government and businesses. Children may not be able to differentiate between the white people at their parents' job that may be giving their parents a hard time, and the white teacher or principal teaching them. For example, children may begin to say things like, "I hate my teacher because she's white. She doesn't like me because I'm black. This school is racist. I'm failing because these people are prejudice." Once children adopt this point of view, their desire to learn in that system begins to fade away. They begin to rationalize their behavior and suggest that school is not a place where blacks can be successful. That it's a place only for whites, or for blacks that are "sell outs."

Indeed, this type of thinking is not only unproductive but is extremely disturbing. As a teacher, I witness high performing students being ostracized and denounced by their peers, being made fun of, picked on and laughed at. All the while, those that are doing the ridiculing continue to read two and three years behind their counterparts, continue to fail, and continue to view school as an insignificant road through life's travels.

I also remember working in an integrated school, and hearing students complain about the teachers not treating them fairly. I further remember teachers saying, "I was called a racist by my student." I do believe there were occasions where the school was not sensitive to the needs of the black students, and where the school was simply not accustomed to dealing with black students, therefore overlooking them. However, on many occasions, the teachers were accused of things that they had no part in. Some were called racist and they weren't. Parents contributed mightily to students being combative, or unfairly blaming teachers, when they complain in front of their children about the injustices and problems they face at work, or in society as a whole.

I'm not minimizing the problems blacks face because I faced them, and continue to face them. Indeed, all blacks face a great deal of adversity, notwithstanding their social economic status. Nevertheless, when children hear parents complain about white people, they begin to generalize and paint all white people with the same brush.

It is, therefore, imperative that parents not share with their children all the problems and adversities they face; and when they do, try not to bring race into the conversation. Give children a chance at being successful in life. They will have to work along side whites as they grow up. They'll have white teachers, white principals, white bosses, and white peers. If black parents routinely tell their children that the enemy is white, or talk negatively about them, where does that leave that child? In others words, he will have difficulty going to school, and getting along, with them. It sets that child up for failure and a long history of dealing ineffectively with people. As we all know, being able to work with people that are different is so essential in the world today.

A further problem is that it frees that child of any responsibility at school for doing poorly. If his grades are poor, the child will often say, "It's because the teachers don't like me, or they are out to get me." It further suggests that no matter how hard that child work, his accomplishments will be minimized by whites. The child's response is, "Why work hard? It doesn't matter anyway." As I mentioned above, they begin to rationalize their poor behavior and their poor grades. They no longer feel responsible for doing well in school.

I remember taking an administrative class for my principal's certificate. I was part of a group that included two blacks and three whites. I was the only black male student. We were all sharing some of our success stories and failures as teachers. One white male high school teacher didn't understand why so many of his black students weren't taking school seriously. He talked about them not turning in their homework, being content with average to below average grades. As he continued to talk, it registered to me that he wanted me to explain why students that live in solid middle class communities, where the average property value is well over $100,000 don't take school seriously. After all, they aren't poor, nor are they lacking resources, such as books, and computers. I simply responded that money and class aren't always the answer as to why students do well or poorly in school. I didn't go any further with this topic. I changed the subject to something else. But, as I drove home, the conversation really stuck with me. I thought about how whites must view blacks that have access to all the necessary resources, but fail to take advantage of them. Certainly, they know we are more than capable of doing the work because there are some that are doing well. What do they see as the cause? What suggestions do they have?

    I wanted to talk in length about this to him. However, I didn't want him to see me as an apologist for blacks, nor someone who has all the answers. I was, indeed, torn. In retrospect, I think I could've given him some insight as to how to work effectively with black students and parents. However, I got the feeling that, he didn't want that. He wanted me to state that many of these students were not receiving the proper up bringing and were headed for trouble. I didn't know those students; therefore, I really couldn't comment in depth about them.

I did reflect in my mind about my own household. Thinking about things I may be doing that may hinder my child in the future. Through talking with people, and evaluating my own household, it became clear that often times when whites are mentioned in the home, they are discussed in ways that are trivial, even when we are joking. I rarely talk in a way that belittles them or blames them for the plight of blacks. However, I may joke about them in a playful way.

That is, indeed, wrong. Children are not always able to tell the difference. This playful gesturing is just as wrong as directly calling white people names, because it's stereotyping. Impressionable minds don't need to hear that type of talk. Simply put, it has no value. I challenge black and white parents to put an end to this type of talk around the house. When watching television, a movie, or reading the newspaper, be careful about what you say. The more we focus on not saying negative things about people of other races, the easier it gets. We shouldn't feel the minds of our children with information that is stereotypical and unfavorable to others.

In closing, black parents, we must not let our children off the hook. We must have high expectations, require that they strive hard in school, prioritize their obligations, and practice self-discipline. Suggesting that whites are our greatest problem is sending the wrong message. Indeed, racism exist, but it doesn't answer all the questions as to why many of our children are not working hard in school to be the best student they can. In fact, racism should be the motivation behind why black children should work hard in school.

Video Games

Video games are quite popular. When I was growing up, we played video games as well. Fortunately, the games back then were not as addictive as the games are today. The graphics and sound effects are so real. It's very easy for children to play these video games for hours at the expense of doing their homework. Sometimes, I even sit with my son to play the games. It's amazing how much time passes when you're playing.

Unfortunately, it has been my experience, as a teacher, that many students are more concerned with playing video games than reading. A student will tell me that he wasn't able to do his homework for various reasons. As the day goes on, I'll over him talking to his friends about the video game he played with after school or late at night. Now, if this pattern continues for years think about how far behind this student will become compared to his peers.

I'm not suggesting that these games are inherently bad or that they shouldn't be played with. In fact, some of the games are quite educational. However, there is no substitute for students sitting at home working quietly on their schoolwork. I feel okay in saying it can be boring at times. Students are not going to want to study on many occasions. When you tell them to turn the television off, or put down the video game, they may become irritated. That's okay. Anything worth having will take hard work to acquire. Furthermore, parents, if you regulate children's habits early in life, they won't be as resistant when they're told to do their homework, or read for pleasure as they get older. In fact, they'll begin to do it on their own. I believe video games are becoming a detriment for poor students. So many don't desire to read or take the initiative to learn on their own. The problems are compounded when there is something as trivial as a video game competing for their interest. Parents must do a better job at making sure that the time to play these games is regulated. It will benefit the child tremendously.

Good Citizenship

Another essential thing black parents can do for their children, particularly their male offspring, to improve their performance in school is to constantly remind them about their role in society, and how they can be productive in it.

This starts first with explaining and demonstrating what "good citizenship" is. The benefits of working, voting, going to school and listening to authority figures, all fit under the umbrella of "good citizenship." They are all areas that black parents should discuss with their children. The first three are self-explanatory. Most people would agree that there are plausible reasons for working, voting for people that can better serve your interest, and going to school to take care of yourself.

The last area is a little less clear. What does it mean that black parents should teach their children to listen to authority figures? As a teacher, I witness on a daily basis black children working hard to demonstrate their antipathy towards authority figures. Many of them demonstrate their resistance by being rude, overly aggressive towards teachers, administrators and their peers, and not turning in assignments, even those they can do quite well.

The questions that beg for consideration are as follows: why do black children need to be taught the value of following the rules set forth by authority figures? Why do so many teachers struggle with disciplining them?

When I was in elementary school, and high school, teachers were perceived in a positive light. When a child went home to complain about a teacher, the parent would often say, "So what did you do?" Or, "What role did you play in this situation?" Now, it's quite different. When children complain about teachers, parents are quick to side with the child even before listening to all the facts. After this happens on a number of occasions, the child begins to realize that he can always blame the teacher when he's not doing well in school.

In talking to many teachers, they complain tirelessly about having poor relationships with parents and not knowing what to do to improve it and how the parents have formulated opinions about the teacher based solely on what the child says. This type of behavior on the part of the parents has to stop if they want their children to value education and begin taking it more seriously. Black parents must begin to communicate the importance of following the rules that are laid out. Once black children begin to accept the rules, they improve the likelihood of becoming successful in those institutions, by adopting the values, customs, and ways of these institutions.

That does not mean that people will always agree with the rules prescribed by the organization; however, when you challenge them, the proper procedures should be followed. Being defiant and reckless only hurts the doer in the long run.

As a black male, I can attest to having unfortunate things happen to me not always because of what I did, but because of who I am. Being passed over for a job, stopped by the police for no apparent reason, are all unforeseen unfortunate events that have happen to me. My response wasn't reckless and self-defeating. I fought back by going through the proper channels. For children that's not always easy to do. Nevertheless, if parents routinely talk to their children about this, they (children) will begin to get better at it. Following the rules would be second nature.

Until the majority of black youth learn this vital principle, many won't enjoy success in the institutions they work and go to school in. They will continue to drop out of school at relatively high numbers, compared to whites, and begin to show their contempt for school at the elementary level. The status quo means accepting the overrepresentation of black males in our penal institutions, relatively high drop out rates for black males in high school and a continued dislike for education. This can be changed.

Parents Practice Good Citizenship

Children are always watching and listening to what their parents do. How we conduct ourselves impacts how they develop and perceive things early in life. I think we can all agree that when children get off to a good start early in life, their chances of being successful increase tremendously. Things such as paying your bills on time, voting, and reading are all important task that go along way in teaching children about individual responsibility. Many black children are operating at a deficit when it comes to these areas.

Paying Your Bills

It's not easy to have good credit. Job stability seems to be a thing of the pass. Downsizing, company mergers, and job outsourcing all contribute to this feeling of vulnerability at the workplace. Pay increases are not keeping pace with inflation. High utility bills, food prices, and the cost of automobiles appear to be rising daily. When looking at the totality of all these things, it's understandable why the credit rating of many people is suffering. How we cope with these matters is that we often avoid creditors by not answering the phone, yelling, and even swearing at them, when we do. All the while, our children are watching. When we avoid our responsibility in such a palpable way, children are learning that if it's okay for mom and dad to do it, it's acceptable for me as well. This can carry over to their schoolwork, and promote a feeling of indifference towards their schoolwork.

    I'm not in any way suggesting that it's easy to pay bills on time, or that parents don't work diligently to do it. What I am suggesting is that we work even harder to do so, and when you talk to that creditor remove yourself from the presence of your child, and then discuss the matter. Try not to become belligerent on the phone but remain professional. Furthermore, don't let the phone ring incessantly. Think about what must be going through your child's mind. Even though these incidents may appear innocuous in terms of its affects on the child, it's sending the message to the child that mom and dad are irresponsible. I would suggest that parents turn down the ringer if they have to. Give creditors only your cell phone number. What ever you do, don't play hide and seek with creditors in front of your children.

Voting

    Generally speaking black Americans vote less than whites. Many of us don't vote for various reasons. Feelings of indifference and the idea that our plight is not going to improve if we vote or not vote are two main reasons why I believe many blacks don't participate in voting. This feeling of apathy has a negative impact on our community for numerous reasons. First, it almost guarantees us that elected officials won't have to concern themselves with implementing policies that may benefit us because we didn't put them in office anyway. Second, it sends a message to others that we feel powerless. Therefore, when we are mistreated at the workplace, and discriminated against in the housing industry, no one cares because we don't care enough about our on situation to fight back by voting. Lastly, and arguably the most essential point is that, the lack of voting sends a negative message to children, one that suggest that blacks are not a part of the mainstream, can't and will not as a whole prosper in America. Black children rap themselves around this identity because they see it being demonstrated to them when parents complain about their plight, but do very little to improve it. The next step is to say, why try? Many of our youth quit trying early in life. They are seeking other means to survive. Unfortunately, these alternatives continue to have a deleterious effect not only on their individual lives, but our community and our neighborhoods.

Perhaps this can change if every child was taught at home that the right to vote wasn't gained easily by blacks. That many people died fighting trying to gain this right. When we don't exercise this right, we do a great disservice to our predecessors. We devalue its strength, and make all the sacrifices they made in order to give us this right insignificant.

Students hear messages like this often, either at school or on television. I believe, however, that it's not being communicated at home enough. Students need to hear about this issue at home from time to time. It can be easily taught at home by giving children an opportunity to vote on various issues at home, such as what snack to purchase for the house, or which cousin should be visited on a particular holiday. Parents should allow them to vote on issues like this, and stick to what ever they choose. This gives the children an opportunity to see how powerful voting is.

On occasion, I would recommend that parents take the right to vote away from them so they can understand how precious it is, and how different life would be if they didn't have any say so about how they should live.

Also, during state, federal or local election time, I would show a video about how life was in the 1950s and 1960s when blacks where trying to vote in some places. I would focus on the extent to which some people went to prevent this from happening.

Lastly, explain that women, no matter what hue, were not allowed to vote until the 1920 in America. Remind them that women to were treated not like full citizens as well.

Indeed, many of these lessons are taught at school, but when it's done at home or talked about in general on a fairly regular basis, children will be able to identify with it more. Often times, when I'm teaching about a topic in class, students will say, "We talked about that at home." Or, "My mom mentioned that to me when she heard about it on the news." What these students are doing is referencing their home life and comparing it to what is being talked about at school. The more these two places are similar, the more information a child learns, and the more things they relate to and remember.

It goes without saying that voting is the most important means by which individuals can demonstrate their frustration with the status quo. In short, it is the most potent tool we have to improve our lives. It's imperative that children learn this at a young age, so they can strive to do well in school, behave properly in their neighborhoods, and work to be good citizens.

Reading

The importance of teaching your child to read at an early age can't be emphasized enough. Most people agree that reading to them at an early age bolsters their chances of being good readers as they grow up.

Unfortunately, in the black community, reading isn't emphasized enough. Yes, we talk about it a great deal discussing in great length how essential it is. However, when it comes to test scores, it indicates that we are significantly behind our counterparts. Many schools across America, that are racially integrated, are struggling mightily to raise the reading test scores of black students.

The obvious question is, "Why do black students struggle so mightily in Reading?" The argument that standardized test scores are racially bias is not going to be entertained here. Yes, there is a great deal of validity to this argument. However, black children can do better than what they are doing. The mainstream culture is not going to change. In other words, it is not going to adjust to the ways and customs of blacks. We have to adjust to it, if we plan on being successful. That doesn't mean being a "sell out" or forgetting who you are. We must remember and be proud of our heritage. I'm simply saying that the values of the mainstream culture are what all people who desire to be successful must adjust to.

Teaching in an urban setting for most of my teaching career gives me a great deal of insight in this area. I struggle a great deal with motivating my students to read, particularly by black males. Providing incentives, literature circles, time on task techniques are some of the things I do to improve my students' reading skills. I've had some success, and I hope to have more.

It has been my experience that the main reason why reading presents a challenge to black students, and is not readily embraced, is because their home environment, generally speaking, isn't promoting the practice. Many black parents aren't modeling the practice. I've asked many parents, during the time I've been teaching, "What books are your children reading outside of school?" Many times the parents aren't sure. What that tells me is that the parents aren't going to the library checking out books for themselves. If the parents were, there's a good chance they would be able to see what type of book their children were checking out, or be more interested in what their children are reading.

If parents don't value reading, neither will most children. Black parents have to start with changing their behavior as it relates to reading. What I mean by that is, we have to start reading regularly when our children are young. It's not merely enough to simply read the newspaper or the magazine. Books should be the main thing being used. Next, black parents should frequent the library on a regular basis with their children. Set a time during the week and go as a family. Make sure you allow time for your children to check out books. Get involved and interested in what they are reading. Even read the same books your children are reading. Then discuss it with them. Lastly, develop a library at home. Make sure you buy a wide variety of books that interest them. Designate time through out the year for them to read.

Schools are under great pressure to raise test scores. They are doing a lot of innovative things to improve reading. They are having some success. However, many black students are still significantly behind. Schools can only do so much. It is essential that parents begin to model the behavior they want their children to carry out. Talking about it isn't enough. Children must see it be displayed on a consistent basis. When parents do fall short, and behave in a way that is not favorable, get back in there and do better. In my years of teaching, students have taught be that they have this ability to discern what the quality of a person is. They forgive genuine mistakes made by adults. Therefore parents, when you do error unintentionally, strive to correct it and do better. Your children will appreciate it.

As I end this section, let me state that many black parents are already doing the things I discussed above. In many school districts, and communities across America, parents and teachers are working hard to raise student test scores. In my school district, we've had a great deal of success, particularly at the intermediate and primary level, raising test scores. And, parents have a lot to do with our success. I just wish more parents did the necessary things that are required, in order for their children to be successful. I believe without question that the argument that black kids don't test well because state test are racially bias is no longer acceptable. Black children can do well, if their environment promotes the right behavior. We as adults can change the behavior of black youth, if we change ours.

Promptness

There is a saying that blacks have their own time clock. It is intimately called, "colored people time." This means that blacks have accepted the label that they are unable to arrive at a destination on time because of the color of their skin. Moreover, they have accepted the belief that they are less than others in this area.

As a teacher, I see this practice being cared out on a routine bases, when it comes to turning in work on time or being prompt for school. When I was teaching in the inner city, many of my black students tended to be late for school and late turning in their homework. This practice happens because they watch their parents doing some of the same things. I remember having a class where some students came in late a lot. I talked to them daily about the importance of being prompt. Usually, the conversations were conducted in a nonthreatening way. I would say my part and they would normally respond that they were going to improve, or they would remain silent. On one occasion, it didn't quite play out this way. In fact, the conversation got really heated and the student stormed out of the class. I went to talk to the student in an effort to calm her down. The only justification she gave me for being late was that, she operates on "cp time." I begin asking her the following questions: "Do I come to work late? Does the principal have to talk to me about being prompt?" She answered no to both questions. Then I said, "cp time," is not about blacks in general, it's about you. I'm black and I take pride in being on time. I went on to say that "cp time" was an excuse people used because they aren't organized and responsible, and that it didn't have anything to do with being black.

Labels like this appear harmless, but they can influence impressionable minds. When kids begin to adopt these values, it only sets them up for failure. What good is it to suggest that blacks operate off of "cp time?" What's the rationale behind it?

These behaviors are hurting black children in school. They're not learning the value of being on time and about responsibility. This will hinder them as they get older, and seek employment.

Black parents must demonstrate how to be prompt to their children, along with the reason why it is so essential, if they are going to learn it. Certainly students are admonished at school, and hopefully it teaches them to do better. However, schools are not in as good a position as parents to teach values. The relationship the child has with the parent is, for the most part, a loving and nurturing one; therefore, the child is more likely to trust and revere the advice coming from the parent more than that coming from a teacher or an administrator. That's not to say that students don't listen to teachers and administrators. They do, indeed, listen and they learn a great deal from them. However, long lasting values are better taught at home. Besides the reason mentioned above, students generally spend on average six hours a day in school, as opposed to eighteen hours at home. Therefore, it's quite understandable why the latter is more influential.

Career Choices

When I ask many of my black students what they want to be when they grow up, the response I often get is, "I don't know," from the girls. From the boys I generally get, "a basketball player," or a "rap star." It always bothers me when I hear students respond as such. It indicates that they haven't been exposed to people working in different occupations enough and that they're not talking about their future to their parents in a serious way.

It's been my experience that many black girls have some idea as to what they want to be when they grow up, but they are a little coy about sharing it. When I talk to them individually, or in small groups, they normally share what their long-term plans are. Often times, it ranges from being a cosmetologist to being a lawyer or a nurse. When they respond with these answers, I support them and reassure them they have the ability to do it.

Unfortunately, the response from the black males is the same when I break them up into groups or talk to them individually. They typically are more limited in scope and more unrealistic. Becoming a professional basketball player or a rapper is unlikely to happen. The latter has a lot to do with the glamorization of the rap lifestyle that's seen on television. From the expensive jewelry, luxurious cars, big homes and beautifully endowed women are all depicted on television.

Furthermore, the lyrics, and in some songs the rebellious lyrics rappers extol, are embraced by many black youth. It's like they're living vicariously through rappers because some of them (youth) feel angry or bitter about their circumstances.

Telling a child that becoming a rapper is wrong should never happen for three reasons. First, children like to do the opposite of what you say. If you want to persuade them, try to use no as little as possible. Secondly, becoming a rapper is not a bad thing. It's only entertainment. Many rappers have not lived the life they are talking about. They're just selling records. Third, it's a profession that is very profitable. Many rappers make a honest living doing something they enjoy. It's similar to acting.

The main cause for concern I have regarding the strong desire black male youth have for becoming rappers or basketball players, is when they focus only on these two occupations at the exclusion of other career choices. It doesn't take a formal education to become a rapper. If youth limit their options to rapping, it follows that they may not aspire to do well in school; and, there's the problem. Everyone understands that the likelihood of becoming a rapper or a professional basketball player is highly unlikely.

When students tell me that they want to be a basketball player, I respond with, "What are you going to do if you don't make it?" When I challenge them a little further, they normally start listening. Here's an example of how the conversation normally goes:

>**Me**: What do you want to be when you grow up?
>**Student**: A basketball player.
>**Me**: What happens to you if you don't make it?
>**Student**: I'm going to make it.
>**Me**: The average NBA player is about 6'4. One thing you can't determine is how tall you're going to be.
>**Student**: But look at Allen Iverson, he's short and he made it.
>**Me**: Well, Allen Iverson isn't that short. He's about 6'0, which is taller than the average male.
>**Student**: Well, I'm going to be tall.
>**Me**: You don't know for sure; so why not prepare to be something else just in case you don't make it to the NBA?

Once again, youth are impressed with the lifestyle of athletes. Many of the material things I described rappers as having also applies to athletes. This is, indeed, where parents must get involved. They have to find ways to expose their children to people who work in different occupations. For whites, it's much easier because in their families there's a greater likelihood of having people that work in various occupations. For blacks, particularly the poor, it's less likely that they'll have these readily accessible role models.

Black parents should join groups; get involved in different programs at school, at church, and in their communities or outside of it, in order to expose their children to different people. When children are exposed to different things, it increases the choices they have in life. Therefore, it improves their chances of being successful.

I remember having career day when I was teaching in the inner city. I had about two guest that came, both were black men, one was a judge, the other was a stockbroker. The students were impressed with both, particularly the latter. They had heard of blacks being judges before, even though they didn't have any in their families; however, not one student heard of a black person being a stockbroker. In fact, only two students knew what a stockbroker was.

If students don't know the choices that exist in life, what's the motivation to study hard? What's the motivation to study challenging subjects? What's the motivation to not sell drugs? What's the motivation to not drop out of school? What's the motivation to care about school?

Chapter II
Decreasing the Achievement Gap

There's a crisis in our public school system that is getting worse. It's a situation that people often talk about, schools spend thousands of dollars trying to improve and unfortunately the results are not improving fast enough. I'm referring to the poor academic performance of many of our black male students, particularly those in poor communities. In my experience, having worked in all black schools and integrated schools, the students that were performing the worst were typically black males relative to black girls, white males, and white females. In my discussions with many of my colleagues that teach in all black schools, and racially integrated schools, there is great difficulty in improving the academic performance of black male students. Black males are more likely to have lower scores in Reading and Math compared to the three listed above.

In further discussions with teachers, they routinely state that black males were more likely to have problems behaving appropriately in class. Teachers were hard press to come up with ideas to motivate the students to do better and begin to take school more seriously.

The question that needs to be asked is, "Why do black males have more difficulty in school relative to black girls, and whites in general? In part 1, I wrote about the things I think black parents can do to help their children do better in school. In part II the areas I'll be focusing on include four solutions that I believe would help black male students improve their academic and behavior output in school: changes in hiring practices, educational forums, creating vocational/cooperative schools in areas with relatively sizeable high school dropout rates, and creating residential public schools.

In the 1950s, Abraham Moslow advanced our thinking about motivation. Moslow believed that "human life" will never be understood unless its highest aspirations are taken into account (Hanson, 197).

Moslow argued that human motivation can be broken into five basic categories of needs: (1) physiological, (2) safety, (3) social, (4) esteem, (5) self-actualization (Hanson, 197).

Physiological needs: This consists of basic survival needs, such as food, air, water, sex, shelter, and sleep (Hanson, 197)

Safety needs: When the physiological needs are meet then this becomes especially important. It included protection of job security, protection from danger, illness, economic disaster and the unexpected in general (Hanson, 197).

Social needs: This is a desire for a worker to have friendship, feel that they belong and feel connected to their peers (Hanson, 197).

Esteem needs: This is the need for self-confidence achievement knowledge and independence (Hanson, 198).

Self-actualization: This is the need Moslow states is behind the drive to become everything a person is capable of becoming (Hanson, 198).

According to Moslow, in order to move successfully up each stage, the one preceding it must be met. In other words, the needs of each stage must be met in order for the person to move to the next step. If that doesn't happen, the ultimate stage, which is self-actualization, will never be met, self-actualization means, in this context, achieving high grades.

It has been my experience that far too many black male youth aren't motivated to excel in school. Many seem so disinterested at a relatively young age. This negative approach to school will only hinder them as they matriculate through the school system. It will result in inappropriate behavior in school, perhaps joining gangs and eventually even dropping out of school. According to the U.S Department of Education, National Center for Education Statistics in 2001, 13% of all black males 16-24 dropped out of high school. For white males in the same age group, it was 7.9%. The ratio is almost 2 to 1. It's been my experience that apathy starts in elementary school.

Every year, I 'm normally proud of what I accomplish with most of my students. As the end of the school year draws near, I tend to think long and hard about my successes and failures throughout the year. I can say without equivocation that black males present the toughest challenge. I've won awards from my principal for my innovations in the classroom. I've been recognized by my colleagues for being a good disciplinarian. I've also been praised by many parents for helping their sons do better in school. Even still it's a tremendous challenge motivating black males to do well in school.

As Moslow maintains, until basic needs are met, self-actualization or the desire to get high grades in school will not happen. Unfortunately, many young black males living in single-family homes headed up by women feel unsure and insecure about their plight. If a ten year old feels that he is the man of the house, the pressure on that child is tremendous and, indeed, cumbersome.

When I do home visits of some of my students, I see first hand why so many black male youth are less interested in school than others. Many of them express that they are worried about the financial situation in the home and how it affects their mother and younger siblings. Many of them have told me that when they do turn eighteen, they'll get a job, and take care of their family. Often times my response is, if you don't receive a quality education, the type of job that you will get will not be enough to take care of a family. And, there's the problem. Many of them are trying to fulfill the role that their fathers should be fulfilling.

Issues involving safety concerns also impact the mind set of many black male youth. Being the oldest, or the only male in the house, means they're the protector, or at least they are in their minds. Particularly when the males live in high crime areas, they feel added pressure to protect their mother and siblings from harm. After all, crime is much higher in these areas.

I remember visiting a former student of mine. He was a good student, but he had the tendency to daydream a lot. As the work became more difficult, daydreaming became a liability. I visited his home to talk to his parents about it. What I found out was that there wasn't a father in the home. My student was the oldest out of three siblings. He had to baby sit them immediately after school, and cook dinner. He also had to do his homework and help them with theirs. During the late evening, he had to walk to the bus stop to pick up his mother, when she got off work because it was dark outside. This daily routine was a lot for a twelve year old. It was quite clear to me why he daydreamed so much in school. He had a lot on his mind; so much that, he had difficulty focusing on his schoolwork. He expressed to me on a number of occasions his concern for their safety, as well as his. He talked about the number of fights he had around the neighborhood, and how he was compelled to fight for survival. When he talked to me, I could see the fear in his eyes as well as the determination to make it in an environment that was tough. His concern for his mother was not only genuine, but mirrored that of an adult. He had assumed the role of the man of the house, and the mother allowed him to because she needed his help. Again, this was overwhelming for a twelve year old.

The feeling of belonging is the next step in Moslow's hierarchy of needs. In the context of the school setting, it has been my experience that many black males feel disconnected from the school system. Many appear to be bored and disinterested in what is being taught. Many, therefore, seek to form alliances with their peers in the form of gangs, in an effort to compensate for their unfavorable relationship with the school system. This leads to more problems in school such as, bad behavior, low grades, and eventually quitting school all together.

The final stage is self-actualization, which is achieved by being rebellious, the class clown, a tough guy, or "Mr. Cool." I remember talking to one of my former students about how he thinks his peers view him. I started off by saying, "You want to be popular with girls, but how popular do you think you are with so many failing grades?" His response was, "They love me." I said, "What do you mean?" His response was, "They think I'm cool because I always get in trouble." Unfortunately, he was right. He was very popular and admired for being disruptive and noncompliant. For far too long, many black youth have been supporting this rebellious type of behavior where studying and good grades are frowned upon, and speaking negatively to those students that are "good" students.

I'm quite sure this wasn't the type of self-actualization Maslow was referring to, but it does describe the type of thinking and behavior that is taking place in so many schools heavily populated by black males. The question that follows is how do we change this pattern of behavior? How do we get black male students to do better in school?

Maslow's normal hierarchy of needs isn't being met by many black boys in our public school system. As a result, many aren't self-actualizing. Put another way, black boys are not getting what they need in traditional school settings in order to be successful. I believe they can, if the public school system can make some adjustments.

These ideas I have will work to bridge the gap between what black boys are capable of and what they are actually achieving. They are based on my experience in the classroom, and the many conversations I've had with fellow teachers, administrators, parents and professors during my teaching career. I've had the pleasure of working in predominantly black schools, racially integrated, and economically diverse schools, along with alternative schools. This broad experience gives me a great deal of insight in to what many schools are experiencing, and why so many are frustrated with the performance of many black boys.

Hiring Practices

There needs to be an improved commitment by school districts to hire more black male teachers in poor inner city schools. The reason is because these schools typically have more students that are being raised in single-headed households, headed up mostly by women. There are two reasons why black men would improve the academic performance of these students.

First, they serve as role models. Many of my black male students need a positive black male role model that they see on a regular basis. In many of their communities, they see so many negative influences, far too many black men not working, and far too many young black male adults hustling illegally. Black male teachers provide balance for these students, in terms of their perception of black men. The stereotype that define black men negatively could be questioned by these students because they'll see some who are working every day, raising a family, and paying taxes.

As a black male teacher, I'm often in the minority. I don't come into contact with many black male teachers. It's unfortunate because I believe many would take the approach that I have, which is to embrace the identity of being viewed as a role model. Not only do I proudly wear this label, I work hard to live up to it. I make sure that I'm careful about what I say to my students when we're casually talking. I talk extensively about being self-reliant, family values, treating people with respect, careers choices, good citizenship, and doing positive things in the community. Also, I almost always wear a tie or a sports coat to demonstrate some professionalism.

I've had many of my former male students' say, "I wish I could live with you." Or, "I wish I had a father like you." That's not to say that I'm this great person with all the answers because that couldn't be further from the truth. I am quite average in every respect. However, I am a black male that they see on a regular basis who tries hard to live the right way. Students have the ability to be able to determine if their teacher is someone of good character because they are very observant and watchful.

The second reason deals specifically with self-identity. As I stated earlier, many black males seem disinterested in school at a relatively early age. It's been my experience that at the fourth and fifth grade, they begin to exhibit many problems academically and behaviorally. Furthermore, many don't foresee themselves working in careers that require a formal education. It is at this level where some of the schoolwork begins to get more challenging and the teachers move a little faster. When many of black male students face adversity in their schoolwork, they say, "I can't do it." Or, "it's too hard." It is at this point that I begin to push them harder, and work them a little more in an effort to get them over the hurdle. When they see a black male who is able to teach them about literature, algebra, or history, it communicates to them that the information can be learned by someone other than a female or someone white. I often tell my black male students, "I was just like you growing up. I loved sports and loved joking around; however, the difference between me and you was that I loved doing well in school." When they see someone who looks like them, and once acted like them, at least to some degree, they identify with that person more. I've had many black male students do a complete turn around in terms of their academic achievement. At one point, some were not serious students, but after watching my actions, and observing my resolve they began to turn around. They soon realized that what I expected from them was nothing less than their best. The idea that learning is for everyone began to sink in.

    I do believe that some of this success had to do with the fact that I am a black male and many of my students could identify with me. Perhaps they saw me as a father figure, a role model, and someone they wanted to be like. In either case, I was able to influence them.

In short, I do believe that communities that are starved for positive black male role models need to start first with getting more black male teachers. It would serve them well.

Educational Forums

Being that the average school day is about six hours long, students typically spend 4.5 to 5 hours working on different subjects. The other hour is spent on lunch, study hall, or recess. Schools that are struggling with discipline, gang activity, low test scores etc... could benefit from a program I call Educational Forums. The Forum Model is a combination of a traditional school day being carried out in a normal way with part of the day focusing solely on counseling, mentoring and advising students on areas such as, careers, drugs, sex, self-esteem, problem solving techniques, self-esteem issues and behavior management. The curriculum that is developed for traditional subjects can also be developed for these areas. It is because of these areas that so many black students, particularly the males, are losing interest in education.

The Forum Model could be implemented in a six hour school day, where four hours are spent teaching traditional subjects, half an hour for lunch, and 90 minutes devoted to teaching the aforementioned areas. The latter should be taught in a non-traditional way. Traditionally, teachers are givers of information and they lead the discussion. In the Forum Model, students would take a more active role, leading discussions and different exercises. Counselors and professionals from many areas would be brought in to facilitate some projects. Trips to different job industries would be at the forefront of this program. Many students in poor areas don't get to see people working in different occupations.

The Forum Model puts just as much focus on academics than it does the social and mental developmental areas. The areas of academics are not the only areas that should be focused on with students. There is quite a bit more; so many of them need valuable information on real world things, and issues that are presently affecting their lives. Thus, many of them struggle with peer pressure, in the areas of sex, gangs and drugs, or just rebelling against school because they are bored.

We can't pretend that the youth are not having problems in these areas. Nor can we pretend that these issues are not affecting their lives. We must do something about it.

Vocational/Cooperative Schools

In talking and listening to many high school administrators and teachers in Chicago, on any given day they may have 30 to 40 percent of their students not in attendance. If students aren't in school, what are they doing? If so many students are not going to school, why is that? What is the school system doing about it?

In response to the first two questions, when students aren't in school, they are hanging out in the street. Before I wrote this book, I took a ride through some neighborhoods in the city of Chicago. I saw so many teenage boys on street corners, so many loitering in front of stores, and far too many simply sitting on their front porch wasting time.

Many of them standing on the corners were watching out for the drug dealers to make sure the police weren't around. Some were selling the drugs themselves. Many of these teenage boys go to school, when they feel like it. They decide when to go and when not to.

I recall talking to a Math teacher who works for an inner city high school. He told me that many students have the potential, if they apply themselves. He went on to say that the main problem is their poor attendance. He said that on any given day almost 30 percent of his students may not attend school.

This isn't happening in all or even most of the inner city high schools across America; however, it is happening in some. Something has to be done about it. The question is: What should the school system do to get teenagers to come to school on a regular basis? Put another way, how do we make school meaningful enough to provide the desire for them to come to school? After all, if they aren't in school, they can't be taught. Certainly, some would disagree with these questions and suggest that it is not the job of the school system to make sure students get to school, but to simply teach them. My response is that in a perfect world that would be true. But like I have argued all throughout this book, many children aren't being raised in an ideal setting with positive role models and access to quality resources. Many of them have to find their own way to get by and succeed. As a result, it is essential that schools accept the challenge and find ways to improve the performance of their students.

In answer to the above question, schools have to find a way to implement a curriculum that is more exciting to students, and that will give them job skills upon graduating from high school. I recommend that all inner-city schools with dropout rates of at least 20 percent institute Cooperative Education programs. In this approach, the "students curriculum is adapted to his vocational needs in a particular career" (Task Force, 110). The student is given the option of choosing the career he wants. He mainly takes courses that would prepare him for that career. Cooperative Education is similar to a vocational school in that a traditional form of education is not necessarily sought.

Unfortunately, not enough schools have programs like this. Many other countries, such as Germany, offer apprenticeship vocational type programs for students that aren't concern with attaining a more traditional form of education, or for students who completed high school, but aren't concerned with going to college (Thurow, 275). Indeed, the United States is unique amongst industrialized nations in that high school dropout and non-college bound students in the United States don't have a nationally endorsed program that will prepare them for careers (Thurow, 275). In some respects, the problem is political. Contriving a national program that would require local school boards and the surrounding community to work together may prove difficult. The most difficult question that will be raised is: how will be the program funded?

One possibility is to pass the American equivalent of the French law that requires business firms to invest 1 percent of their revenues in training. "Firms must pay a tax of this amount but can deduct their own internal training costs from this tax" (Thurow, 279). Indeed, "since all firms have to pay for training they must as well train (Thurow, 279).

Schools boards may be ambivalent about such a program as such because they fear that property taxes may be increased. This fear can be put to rest by guaranteeing that property taxes will be indexed to inflation.

However, one area that will not prove difficult is deciding in what schools to implement this program. Schools with excessive dropout rates should be targeted. I recommend 20% be the targeted number. I think most people would agree that 20% is a pretty significant number of students. Thus, if 80% of the students are graduating from high school, those not graduating represent a pretty substantial amount. And, they need to be doing something constructive. If not, they can get in to a whole lot of trouble.

Unfortunately, that's what's happening. Many of those youth that are in and out of jail aren't in school consistently. Apparently, they have given up on acquiring an education. Their resolve is to simply survive. That means doing what ever it takes, such as hustling, and stealing. Certainly, a nation as rich as ours and with some of the best minds in the world can give these struggling teenagers better alternatives.

Cooperative programs that prepare these students with job ready skills would help not only them, but our entire country. So many high tech jobs go unfilled because people don't have the required skills. High tech areas in computers, computer information and manufacturing need people. We have the population available. It's just a matter of teaching them the skills.

The lack of interest in school teachers see exhibited by so many students would decrease, if students know what they are learning will mean getting a quality job in a relatively short period of time, one that pays more than the minimum wage, and one that is the beginning of a career. If such is provided, there is no question in my mind that fewer black teenagers would dropout of school, fewer would be so attracted to selling drugs, fewer would end up in jail or dead, fewer would think at an earlier age that school is for others, and fewer would think being smart means "selling out" or is not cool.

Schools would benefit by having a student body more interested in school, students more willing to study, and less likely to cause disruptions. Test scores would improve. There would be less teacher and administrator turnover rates, less parents worried that their child won't have a future,

Communities would benefit because there would be less drug dealing going on, less youth getting involved in gangs and all the deplorable activity that goes along with being associated with gangs. Residents would no longer feel like they are prisoners in their own homes. They could walk around in their communities and feel safe. Parents could now allow their children to go outside without fearing that they'll be victimized by gang activity.

I believe all of this can be made possible. However, it won't be easy. The challenge is to get federal and state legislatures, businesses, parents, and school officials to support it. Although there are many vocational schools that operate in a similar fashion, as I described, there aren't enough, particularly in the areas that they need to be. Furthermore, the businesses don't play a great enough role so that the students can make a relatively easy transition from school to work. In order for it to work businesses must be a major player in this process. In high tech areas, where there is a shortage of qualified workers, I'm sure they would welcome the invitation.

Residential Public Schools

A fourth recommendation I have that would in my opinion improve the educational achievement of black males is the development of public residential schools. These institutions would educate students the traditional way, meaning six-hour schools etc. However, students would live at these facilities throughout the year.

So many times I've heard teachers say, "I wish I could take this child home with me. He would be a different person." Or, "If I could change this child's environment, he would be totally different. These statements recognize the impact that a child's environment has on his educational success. I don't need to quote statistics to make the case that what children see everyday in their community, in their home, and who they talk to influences the decisions they make. Hundreds and even thousands of books address this issue. I think it's safe to say that most people would agree that raising a child up in a positive environment where education is valued gives a child an advantaged over those that don't have the same quality influences.

Residential public schools would remove many children from unfavorable environments, where gangs, drugs and violence are the norm. It seems that almost everyday you hear on the news or read in the paper about children being shot only because they were at the wrong place at the wrong time. Removing children from these environments will only increase their chances of becoming productive members of society.

Residential public schools don't have to be located in remote areas or rural areas. They could be located right in the inner city. Certainly, critics will argue about issues such as, how to finance these schools, who should attend etc. I'll be the first to say that these are plausible concerns. However, they can be worked out. The benefits of developing these schools, would save a lot of students from getting involved in drugs and gangs, along with other activities that are not beneficial to their educational success.

Thirty years ago no one would have thought that charter schools would be possible. If someone had recommended it, they would've have been laughed at, told that they were misinformed, and that it would be impossible to do. If school vouchers had been mentioned during this time, this to would have been subjected to public scorn.

Indeed, like most new suggestions, they appear to be impossible because it causes us to think in a way in which we are not accustomed to. New ideas are scary because there are always winners and losers, those that benefit and those that don't. However, in the suggestions that I have put forth there are all winners. Everyone would benefit from a school system that improves the performance level of some of the hardest to reach students.

I do understand that trying to implement any of these ideas would be extremely difficult. Legal issues abound, financial, and political concerns abound. My objective is to generate ideas that will give teachers, community leaders, politicians, along with parents, hope about improving the educational performance of all children.

I believe the country is spending so much money and resources on imprisoning people that so much is being taken away from other areas such as education. If we can't continue to fund it like it should be, perhaps the system can be changed in away that will make it more productive. That's not to say that money is irrelevant, or that it can't make the educational system better because to some extent it can. However, even if we continue to fund education to the point that it keeps up with inflation, I don't think that will solve many of the problems that are affecting some of the schools in America. Many of them have problems that go well beyond economics. More money will simply mean more of the same. Indeed, there has to be some recognition that how we are educating many children must be changed, and not solely what we are educating them with.

In conclusion, the four recommendations being offered are not needed in many communities where positive role models exist, where strong family structures are apparent, and where communities are filled with the necessary resources to help youth progress positively. However, in communities where the aforementioned are not readily available, I believe these recommendations can help guide youth, particularly black males, toward a positive future.

Chapter III
Ways to Educate Black Males

Everyone can't be educated the same way. Different strategies and styles must be used to effectively teach students. The one size fits all mentality, or the one best way approach is obsolete. As educators, we must adjust our style to the population we are teaching. If one style doesn't work, try another one. If that is unsuccessful, try a different one. Just like technology is constantly changing, people are as well. And, the people I'm talking about are the students.

Yes, they are changing just has rapidly as technology. The ideas they come to school with are indeed amazing. Years and may be even decades ago, it was acceptable to teach students one-way. Information wasn't coming so rapidly in our society. People weren't required to grasp information so quickly.

Now that time has passed. It is not coming back. This is the information age, where newness is embraced, different ideas are respected, thinking out of the box is encouraged, and brainstorming is popular. Indeed, this must be carried over to our school system. In other words, we must embrace change, not changes that are ineffective, but those that work.

In this section, I will focus on four strategies I use to effectively teach black boys. Although they may not be the strategies that were used in the past, they should, however, be used in the future. And, the future is now. They are as follows: adjust the teaching style to real life events in the lives black boys; teach anger management; make sure the setting is structured and well disciplined; build up the self-image of black male students.

My years of experience as an educator have shown me that to be effective at teaching black male students in inner city schools, and poor schools, I have to tailor my lessons more to their everyday life. In other word, I have to make the lessons come alive.

This is not always easy because there is a certain amount of information students have to memorize and learn simply by reading. Unfortunately, however, in far too many schools all the information being taught is being done in the same manner: students sitting passively by and trying to retain some information.

This approach is less effective for students who are growing up in environments where they have to be assertive and even aggressive at times for survival purposes. Children growing up in these communities, which are quite challenging, have to be taught information differently in many cases in order for it to stick with them and mean something to them.

It's been my experience that relating the information in a real world since promotes better attention and increases their desire to learn. Students are able to identify with it; therefore, they can recall it better and understand faster. For example, if I'm teaching a Math class about sales taxes, I'll give examples about blacks pay a higher price for their goods in inner city communities because of the crime that exist. Or, if I'm teaching a Social Studies class about the rights of citizens, I'll talk about events that happened in their community, where I believe the police might have acted unfairly, or about the times in which they did act appropriately because they were trying to keep the community safe.

The second strategy is to make sure I teach anger management to my black male students. It's been my experience that black male youth are more likely to be aggressive than others for many reasons, which to some degree is beyond their control. I believe that growing up in more difficult situations and in homes without a father around can promote more assertive behavior. Facing adolescence without a father around means you don't have that male figure to talk to during difficult times. Therefore, many young black males learn how to be a man by trial and error. This often leads to poor decisions being made. Poor decisions can lead to aggressive and destructive behavior.

My experience has shown me that when I deal with the reason why students are angry rather than what they did, I get better results in terms of the students improving their behavior. Unfortunately, sometimes, the why is very unpleasant. You may feel inept because you can't always give students what they need. Many times I felt powerless and even frustrated because when a student needed something I couldn't always provide it. However, I was able to forge a better relationship with the student because I knew the root of the problem, and would instruct him to deal with his frustration better.

The extent to which frustration can negatively impact what a student is learning can't be overstated. It has been my experience that inner city schools really need peer programs to help students deal with anger management. Many schools with relatively high test scores, where the community is more economically stable have programs that deal with this area. Far too many schools that need peer management or anger management programs the most have it the least. The reason for it has to do with the tremendous pressure they are under to raise test scores in the areas of Reading, Math, Social Studies and Science. According to the administrators I talked to, the push to raise test scores mean most of the resources have to be focused on those central tasks.

I recall an administrator telling me that I was a "softy" because I thought some of my boys needed counseling. Even though I wasn't a certified counselor, I wanted to volunteer some time after school to talk to them about different problems going on in their lives. Well, I was told I couldn't because it would interfere with my teaching by taking time away from grading papers and record keeping. I remember thinking, if I could counsel some of the students that needed it, I could teach more because I would have fewer interruptions. Me being new to the school, I certainly wasn't going to persist. I just continued to teach without complaining. Even though I had some success, I could've had more.

In retrospect, I wish I had complained more, and been more persistent about helping my students. It was so apparent that many of my boys really needed it. I recall visiting a home and finding out that my most challenging student was one of three boys in the home. His father was estranged and the mother was working tirelessly to provide for the boys. Unfortunately, she didn't have enough time to help them with their schoolwork. My student was having a great deal of difficulty in school. He had failed the same grade twice. One of his siblings was only a year older than him, but three grades higher. The frustrated look and feeling of despair this student exhibited on a daily basis was justified. It was not his fought that his father had abandoned him, nor was it his fault that the school didn't have counselors who could help address some of the problems that were negatively affecting the boy. When I tried to offer help, my suggestions were quickly dismissed.

If the public school system is going to effectively teach black boys, they must incorporate programs into the curriculum that will address the needs of their students. I call it the "thorough approach to teaching." This approach recognizes that the needs of students growing up in difficult and challenging situations are different from the needs of other students. To fail to admit this is erroneous and very costly to the students because they'll grow up unable to control themselves when they get angry. Anybody in society that is not equipped to deal with frustrating events in their lives without getting angry is headed for trouble. After all, life is full of adversities. The ultimate challenge is having the ability to overcome them. It is essential that we teach our children this. If we don't, we are failing them.

This leads me to the third strategy. It is the belief that providing a structure environment where discipline is implemented helps black boys achieve. It has been my experience that black boys respond positively to environments where there is a great deal of structure, particularly when these environments are introduced to them at a relatively early age. I've witnessed many teachers having difficulty with black boys because their classrooms were not structured. In other words, they weren't orderly. Students didn't have any boundaries. They were allowed to act how they wanted, say what they wanted, and do what they wanted. This normally meant the teacher was going to struggle with teaching them.

The question that some of you might have is, shouldn't structure be provided for all children? My response is, yes. However, I believe it has to be provided at a much higher level for children growing up in more challenging situations. As I mentioned above, black boys are often the only male in their household. They are given the power to make life changing decisions at an early age. This, unfortunately, means many of them feel as if they are adults. Therefore, many of them are allowed to do things their own way.

A structured school environment is orderly and disciplined. Children are allowed to be children. They are not given power to make all the decisions as to how they want to study, or if they should study at all. They are given some form of independence; however, the environment is stable and organized. Therefore, the only thing they need to focus on is doing well in school.

The inability to focus at school is sometimes understandable. The situation between what's going on at school and what's going on at home are often at odds. Put another way, the environments sometimes differ so substantially that children have difficulty adjusting. When children are given too much freedom at home and parental supervision is limited, they grow accustomed to behaving almost any way they choose. Some of the behavior may not be acceptable for school. Structure needs to be provided in order to combat some of these problems. The structure I'm referring to includes making sure that all students feel safe to learn, that discipline is enforced on a consistent basis, and all students know what the expectations are for academic success. Discipline and structure allows students to feel comfortable in their surroundings.

My ability to discipline students and provide structure is something I had to learn. Even though I always exhibited potential and never had a class that was out of control, I had to read books dealing with this topic and actually experience it in order to get better. I can say without equivocation that all students appreciate working in an environment that is stable because students respect each other and help each other learn. The students that do well in school appreciate it because they aren't ridiculed for being smart. Students having difficulty like it because they get the help they need, and aren't afraid to say they don't understand something. It promotes a positive and a relaxed environment. Indeed, it's not perfect and problems do arise; however, they can be handled effectively and in a relatively short period of time without the assistance of administrators.

The fourth strategy used to effectively teach black male students is to build up their self-esteem. The feeling of powerlessness is seen so clearly on the faces of black boys I teach. Many of them seem to be lacking confidence in their ability to learn new things. They often sit in the back of the class, pair up with students they believe are smarter and resist being called on to answer questions in front of their peers. When I use to insist on them participating before I began working on improving their self-esteem, they would resist even more.

When I first started teaching, I would ask myself why are so many of my black boys unwilling to participate? My response was to be firmer and more persistent. Often times, I would get into slight arguments when some of them resisted.

I recall going over a Math lesson, and calling on one of my students to come to the chalkboard to demonstrate how he arrived at the answer; his response was, "I don't want to." I said, "Come on you have the right answer just write down the steps you took to get it." He looked at me sternly and just became real silent. At that point, I began to realize that the entire class was watching and I couldn't let him off the hook. So I said, "You better get up there now." He jumped up and went to the chalkboard and purposely put down the wrong answer. For the rest of that day, he was very angry and disappointed with me for challenging him in front of his peers.

Before school let out, I talked to him about the incident. His response was, "I don't like to be called on in front of people" I said, "Why not?" He replied, "I just don't." Well, after observing quite a few of my other black male students, they behaved similarly. They didn't want to be called on or made to answer questions.

It took me at least a couple of years to realize just how insecure some black boys felt about their ability to learn. When it comes to sports, however it's the complete opposite. They typically lead the way and show a great deal of confidence in this area. But, when it comes to education, it's quite different. The question as to why so many young black males feel so insecure about their abilities in the area of education is complex. There are a lot of contributing factors, such as conflicts with teachers, limited parental support in the area of education, and low expectations from teachers and parents. Anyone of these factors could contribute to students not performing well in school, and therefore building up a wall of resistance.

The question is, "How do we stop this? How do we as educators and parents improve the confidence level of black male students? My experience has shown me that there are two ways to do it. Certainly, there are others, but I primarily use two. Fortunately, I've had some success as I work to improve my teaching techniques.

First, I find out the things they like to do outside of class and talk to them periodically about it. I do this because it's essential to forge a connection with all of my students, but particularly black male students growing up in difficult environments. They need more positive reinforcement than other students in less difficult environments. When the student is having difficulty in class, I'm able to smooth it out by talking to him about something he likes to do, therefore diverting attention away from the problem area. I normally do it during lunchtime, during a break in the day, or when they're changing classes.

It's important that teachers realize that they shouldn't communicate with students in an adversarial way. Teachers must lead the way in trying to establish good communication and a quality relationship built on trust and respect from students. If all the dialogue is limited to schoolwork, it makes the relationship too tensed. In some environments that will work well; however, in communities where students don't have enough role models and positive influences, teachers must do more than simply teach.

The relationship I build with my students go along way in motivating them to do better because they began to feel a sense of accountability to me. Furthermore, they begin to respect the relationship between teachers and students and not take it for granted.

The other strategy I use is to give them responsibilities in the classroom. Collecting papers, organizing books, taking the names of students that are behaving well when a substitute teacher is present, and delivering messages to other teachers are all duties I give to my black male students in order to boost their self-confidence. When they perform well, I highly extol them. When they perform poorly, I hold them accountable, but I continue to tell them they can do better.

Allocating responsibilities to students communicate that you have confidence in them. And more time than not, they'll work diligently to not disappoint you.

Both of the strategies I use are done to ultimately improve their grades and their academic success; however, in doing so, I hope to raise their confidence level and get them to believe in themselves.

It's so disheartening to see so many young black boys exhibit low self-esteem, and we as teachers do very little to address it. It's frustrating for me as an educator to see teachers fail to address this issue in their teaching and classroom management techniques. I have seen too much criticism and not enough positive reinforcement. The only thing the former does is that it further communicates to students that are struggling academically that they aren't expected to learn the material because they are incapable.

This failed relationship with teachers begins early in a child's educational career. I've heard many first and second grade teachers speak poorly about many of their students right in front of them. Sometimes it's done because the teacher is angry, not necessarily because the teacher believes it to be true. Nevertheless, the affects are the same. It robs children of their confidence and this leads them to loath school. Then they begin to question their ability.

As a black male, I realize how important it is to be confident in your abilities. Sometimes black men are stereotyped unfavorably and assumed to be associated with many negative things. Often times, it's portrayed in the media in many forms. If I believed everything I heard about black men, I would feel compelled to walk with my head down because of guilt and shame. My sense of knowing who I am and what I'm capable of gives me the strength to denounce these stereotypes and realize they don't apply to me.

Teachers that work in the difficult communities, where most of the homes are headed up by women, where many students don't have a father in their life, and where boys are made to believe that they have to be physically tough in order to become a man, have to realize, as I did, that you must work on improving a child's self-image of himself, in the area of education, in order to effectively teach him.

In no way am I suggesting that teachers have to like all of the students they teach. That's highly unlikely. However, they must have the utmost respect for each and everyone. Respecting them means equipping them with the necessary skills that will aid the students tremendously as they matriculate through school. It's not about how teachers feel, but how we make the students feel. The better we make them feel about themselves, the easier it is to teach them. Confidence can go along way it getting students to perform better. In fact, students can overachieve if they are confident enough in their ability. Teachers often complain about what they don't like to do because of various reasons. But, when you teach students that don't have all the necessary resources like others have, you must go that extra mile. The extra mile may mean giving more time to the job, being more creative, being more flexible and being more understanding. Although it's challenging, it is rewarding.

In conclusion, the four strategies I use are a small sample of many techniques teachers use to effectively teach black male youth. These are the four strategies that work well for me. They enable me to get the most out of my black male students both academically and behaviorally. I've seen some change their behavior in a relatively short time and perform quite well academically, after beginning so poorly. These strategies are universal in their appeal, meaning they can work for other teachers as well. However, simply going through the motions is not enough. It's imperative that teachers believe in the value of the four strategies and understand that the focus should not be on the teachers, but on the students. So even if some of the strategies make teachers feel uncomfortable, or is something they aren't accustomed to doing, if it improves the students' educational output and behavior, it should be used.

In short, educators have an obligation to students and to their parents to provide the best education they can. They may error; however, their resolve should always remain: they should educate all children to the best of their ability. Let me end by saying, these strategies are not a panacea. Students will still get into mischief from time to time. They'll still behave like children do; however, I believe teachers will be able to understand their students better, and keep problems to a minimum. That means the classroom will be more productive.

Chapter IV
The Purpose of This Book

I believe blacks are at a critical point in their lives. There are so many negative things impacting the black community. So many people are feeling disenfranchised and so many people are experiencing hardship. The end result is it's having grave consequences on the lives of black children, particularly the young black boys.

Far too many of them feel discouraged and insecure about their position in the world. They see their brothers, uncles, fathers, cousins and friends being thrown in jail at alarming rates. They see families being torn apart as a result of this, children being raised with only a mother in the home and no positive black male role model present.

They see so many drugs being sold in the communities in which they live, so many family members and friends being killed as a result of drugs. They witness so many drug users standing on the street corners begging for money, homes being broken into by drug users to support their habit.

They see gang members fighting, shooting, intimidating residents from feeling comfortable in their own neighborhoods, vandalizing local merchants, and forcing youth to join the gang.

They see the consequences of poverty and despair on a daily basis, so many black men not working, drinking on the corners wasting time. They see blight in their neighborhoods, stores closing down and youth not working.

They see schools struggling hard to improve the academic performance of students, but in many instances, falling short. They see teachers get angry and discouraged because of the poor behavior and attitude of so many students. They see high teacher and administrator turnover rates, new people coming in and out of their school, many simply leaving because they can't get the results needed to stay.

They see television programs depicting black men and boys in a negative and offensive way, videos supporting drug dealing, hustling to get by and some women supporting this lifestyle. They see very few positive black male role models on television that show black men working everyday and taking care of a family.

In the mist of all of these influences, we wonder why so many black boys aren't concerned with getting an education, aren't concern with thinking positively about their future, aren't concern with working, aren't concern with taking life seriously.

Something on a wide scale has to be done if we are going to change the mind set of black male youth, something that shows we care about the poor choices they are making, something that shows we have had enough of them going in and out of jail because they are shooting each other, destroying neighborhoods by their poor actions, and drug dealing.

As a teacher, I am the first line of defense. I see the affects of the problems they are facing on a daily basis. It's my job to teach them about Reading, Writing, Social Studies, and Math. It's my job to motivate them and provide a spark that will capture their attention. And, it's my job to challenge them to learn as much as they can.

As a black man, it's my job to teach them about life, about making quality decisions that can positively impact their lives. Teaching them about individual responsibility and being accountable to themselves for the decisions they make in life. Showing them how a black man should conduct himself. Showing them that the stereotypes that define black men are not accurate. Showing them that we can't blame society for every problem we incur, particularly if our behavior causes the problem.

In the next section, I am challenging black men to do the same, to change the life for the better of one black male child, to take responsibility for their own actions and improve the life of their families. Indeed, many of you are. I'm referring to those that know they can do better but aren't. I'm also going to address some things I think black women can do to improve the relationship between black men and their sons.

Chapter V
A Teacher's Challenge

When I look at the faces of many of my black male students, a feeling of ambivalence comes over me. On the one hand, I see bright young men with so much potential and so much to offer the world. Even though some may be rough around the edges, they are quite intelligent. Their insight never ceases to amaze me.

Yet, when I talk to some of them to get an understanding as to how they view themselves in the world, so many of them have a negative self- image of themselves and a narrow view of what they have to offer. I call this negative view the "invisible weight." In other words, it's not tangible to the extent that it can be touched, physically carried away, or put in storage; nevertheless, it can be felt either by the person the young man goes in front of to apply for a job, or someone like me, a teacher. This "invisible weight" has so much power and influence because it limits the aspirations, goals, and ambitions of those that carry it around.

The questions that beg for consideration are: how did that "invisible weight" get there? And, how can it be removed?

It's been my experience that, on average, black children see the world differently than white children. The former is more skeptical and more cynical of the world. I see this difference a lot in my classroom when we read novels. It's during this time that students are required to draw on their own experiences in order to understand what's being read. Often times when we as a class are discussing characters in a novel, and a question about the integrity of one the characters is brought up, more times than not my black students are more critical and more cynical about the character.

Quite conversely, my white students, on average, are just the opposite, either they view the character more favorably or they have a wait and see response. The reasons as to why there are differences are many. The environment in which the children live is a factor, the negative images they see black people being portrayed as on television and in movies are factors, and the knowledge that black men are over represented in our jails and prisons is also a factor.

I think it's safe to say that the negative influences are limitless. Unfortunately, the impact they have on the mindset of black young men is also without boundaries. So many of them that I have taught are uncertain about their future, uncertain about where they fit in society, and uncertain about how America as a society views them. This negative self-image bottles up their goals, and puts a lid on them.

My job as a teacher is to remove that lid, and through positive reinforcement, hard work, and praise invoke self-esteem and a desire to look at life more auspiciously. This is, indeed, a difficult task for a teacher. After all, we don't know the ins and outs of every student, their whole background, and the things they've seen in the past that continue to affect them either positively or negatively. In other words, teachers are operating at a disadvantage. Their challenge is to find a way to better connect with that student that is exhibiting high levels of frustration, students that have a negative disposition about themselves and life in general.

To all you teachers, future teachers, and, indeed, parents who after all are the first teachers in a child's life, don't give up on these youth. Many of them are playing the cards they were dealt. Yes, many know right from wrong, and unfortunately routinely choose the latter. But, if we give up on them, what will happen to them? What becomes of society? We can't have youth continue to fall by the waist side, end up in jail, or dead. Things can be done to stop it.

Chapter VI
The Challenge for Black Men

It is time for black men to do better. We make far too many excuses about why we are in the position we are in economically. Some of the excuses are justified, but some aren't. At the same time, some black men can't do better for whatever reason; however, some can. This book is about the latter. It's about communicating directly to those who can improve the plight of their family, improve their relationship with their sons in particular, and work diligently to take back the neighborhoods that have been torn apart by drugs and gangs.

When I taught in the Chicago Public Schools, I worked in an area that was being torn down. The residents were being displaced, given Section 8 vouches, and instructed to seek residency somewhere else. I recall going over a lesson in Math about fractions. As I was introducing the lesson, and giving examples on the board, I recall one student secretly looking down in her lap. This was quite unusual because this particular student was normally very attentive. I casually walked past her and saw a newspaper in her lap as I was going through the lesson. My instincts told me to not address the issue and keep going on with the lesson.

At the end of the day, I mentioned it to her. She stated quite hesitantly that she was looking in the newspaper for apartments that accepted Section 8 tenants. After she said it, she quickly left the room. I quickly sat at my desk and was simply stunned at what I heard. I must have day dreamed thinking about what the student said for about 10 minutes. I recall thinking about how it must feel to be twelve years old and concerned about where you were going to live, and how difficult it must be to study fractions, along with other subjects, when thinking about perhaps not having a place to live, worrying about how the family was going to hold up together with so many things coming their way.

It made me feel that what I was teaching was so meaninglessly. This student was dealing with real life at such an early age. It was at this point that I began to realize that many of my students were going through similar things. Life was not as rosy and full of hope as it was for others. This made me quite sad. I wanted to resign because I felt so sorry for these kids. But, I'm glad I didn't. They taught me a lot about life, and this made a better teacher.

I'm writing about this example to say that everyone doesn't have an equal chance to be successful in life. The road to success is more difficult for some rather than others. However, the year I spent teaching these students showed me that excuses must be held to a minimum because life continues on with you or without you. The tough mindedness and sense of determination these students exhibited, while so many of their friends and relatives were being displaced, illustrated to me that bad times can build character, and, indeed, make you stronger. These students never complained to me about their situations, or even hinted that they wanted me to feel sorry for them.

It was their attitude and mental strength that prompted me to write this book. It showed me that if children can face this much adversity and not give up, we as black men can do better.

Our children are watching. They will do as we do. Unfortunately, our track record is not so good.

The challenge is to work hard to improve the plight of not only ourselves, but also our children. We must welcome the challenge of being role models and embrace it. Making excuses as to why we can't do better is no longer acceptable. Blaming the system for all of our problems is also no longer acceptable. It is time to be more self-reliant, more responsible, and more accountable for our actions.

We must take an active role in motivating our children to do better in school, and better in life. For far too long, we have been sitting on the sidelines allowing black women to take the leadership role. They are exhausted. Furthermore, they get so much resistance from their young sons during their puberty years. It's difficult for women to raise them.

In my years of teaching, I have witness far too many women come up to the school because their sons were misbehaving, and stating, "I can't do anything with this boy. He won't listen to me." My response is normally, "How effective is his father with him?" Often times, the response is, "He doesn't have a relationship with his father." When I hear this, I always say to myself, "That's the problem." Black boys growing up without fathers still continues to be a major enigma in our community.

I'm not going to quote statistics to make the case that fathers need to have better relationships with their father. We can all agree that children benefit more when two quality parents are involved in their upbringing.

It's essential that black men work relentlessly to put an end to this. It's their responsibility to establish a quality relationship with their children. As a black male teacher, I see so many black boys longing for a father and son relationship, and growing frustrated with not having one, as they get older. They exhibit their anger by not doing their schoolwork, lashing out at teachers and administrators, being disruptive and noncompliant at school, and disrespecting the mother because the father is not in the home. The frustration they have is a filling of emptiness. This void stays with them throughout their life.

Indeed, black men, it is time to do better. No more excuses. No more complaining. Our plight, our communities and our families aren't going to improve if we don't accept the challenge to do better. We can change some things if we work diligently and not accept the status quo as being okay.

Chapter VII
What Can Black Women Do To Improve The Relationship Between Fathers And Sons?

It is no secret that too many black women have been raising sons on their own for far too long. Many have done a great job. There have been so many successful black men raised by only their mothers. I applaud these women because I'm sure it was difficult. I do believe, however, that it is even more challenging now to raise sons without fathers in the home. The challenges are different. There are more negative influences today than twenty to thirty years ago. There are so many negative influences competing for the interest of children now days. Parents have to be abreast of so many different things in order to protect their children from these influences.

Furthermore, mothers were able to stay home and better supervise the children because there were more fathers in the home. Now, that has changed. So many women have to work;

as such, children spend so much time alone or with a babysitter. Children aren't getting the feedback they need to make quality decisions because parents are too busy providing a living for the children. Indeed, this analysis is not limited single-headed households. In two parent families, many children spend time alone because it's imperative that both adults work in order to keep pace with the high cost of living.

I hope these difficult challenges send a message to black women that if their son's father is willing and able to establish a relationship with their son support it. I hear so many black men complaining about how they want a relationship with their son, but because they couldn't make the relationship work with the mother, she won't allow them to have a quality relationship with their son.

This destructive type of thinking has to stop, if we are going to make life better for the younger generation. If a father is willing and able to have a relationship with his son, promote and encourage it. Don't make the child suffer for a failed relationship between you and the child's father.

My experience with male students that are in a situation where the mother routinely puts the father down, while he's trying to establish a relationship with the child, means that the child will have academic problems, meaning not turn in work, not participate in class and be quite difficult to deal with.

Anger management problems are responses I've seen these students have. Some tend to get upset relatively easily and have difficulty controlling themselves. I recall talking to one boy's mother about her son getting so upset about the least little thing. Her response was that, "He just misses his father." I asked, "Where is his father?" She said, "He lives in a different city." Well, I was able to get the father's home number. When I was talking to him about his son, the father kept talking to me about the child's mother. He talked in depth about how she won't let him see his son, and about how she criticizes him in front of his son.

After listening to this, and thinking about what the mother said, and then the father, I understood why the child would get so angry. The mother and father were so bitter, and angry with one another. I was certain that when they did communicate with each other, there was a lot of yelling and screaming. When I talked to the father a second time, that's exactly what he said. In fact, he went on to say that he rarely talks to her because it only makes him angrier. I remember thinking, if the father isn't talking to the mother, he probably isn't communicating with the son as often as he would like.

Another problem I've seen male students exhibit in these situations is a tendency to be disrespectful towards their mothers. I believe that happens because, children don't like to hear one parent speak ill about the other. When that happens often enough, the parent that does most of the complaining will feel the brunt of the child's discontent. Because it's normally the mother who is raising the child, she's going to experience more of his frustration. In my experience, the level of disrespect sometimes gets worse as the child gets older. I've seen male students call their mother names, and even hit their mother. I recall working at one school where the administrator had to call the police because the mother tried to reprimand her son by grabbing his arm, and the boy pushed his mother down to the floor. She began crying hysterically. The mother didn't press charges. I've seen other situations where boys not only talked back to their mothers, but called them names, and used profanity towards them. I've had situations where I had to intervene and calm the boys down.

    The responses of the students I described are extremely problematic for these students. It sets them up for failure. It's essential that parents know this and work diligently to stop the war of words and putting each other down.

I encourage mothers to strengthen the relationship between the father and the son. Embrace it. Cherish it. Realize that a child's childhood is short. Lost time can't be made up for. The opportunity the son has to learn important things from the father, during his developmental and teenage years is precious. When that time is over, and if the relationship between the father and son is nonexistent, the child will have missed out on a lot.

There are some very good black men out there that are suffering because mothers are not supporting the relationship between the father and son. At the same time the child is suffering. The challenge for women is to let go of the frustration they may have towards the father. Try hard to not criticize the father in front of the boy. Certainly, it's not easy. But, the more you do it, the easier it becomes. Mothers owe it to their sons to let them have a relationship with their fathers.

As I conclude this section, I'm challenging parents to understand my position as a black male teacher. Believe me when I say that there are far too many black male youth suffering because they don't have a quality relationship with their fathers.

In the black community our families are so broken up, and in so many homes women are raising the boys all by themselves. I want this to improve. I want fathers to have a renewed interest in the lives of their sons, their communities, and their families. I want parents to understand my concern and realize that children are our future. If we don't invest time and effort in them, teach them to get along and coexist in harmony with others without fighting, what type of future will they have? Will they make the same mistakes we did?

The black community can't improve its situation if we are always looking for others to do it. Certainly, some of the problems in the community are not the fault of simply black people. However, there are a number of things we can do differently to stop or decrease the problems we have. We have to want to improve, be accountable for our own actions, and recognize that until we do better, we will not get the respect we often talk about getting.

All the changes must start first with our own families. If we can teach our children about doing right, we can improve. After all, they are the next generation. If not, our plight collectively will only get worse.

Chapter VIII
Conclusion

This book is about the experiences I've had teaching in public schools. It's about the problems I've witness so many children have because of the things they have been subjected to. The reasons for their problems are many, as I outlined above, ranging from problems in the community to that of the home.

I focus specifically on black young males because they are suffering the most. So many are in jail, hanging on the street corners, dropping out of school, and showing a general discontent for school. We are so familiar with data and the research that there is no point in quoting statistics. Everyone reading this book is all too familiar with the state of black male youth in America.

Something has to be done to steer this population back on the right track. I listed numerous things that I think parents can do to improve the lives of black young males. Suggestions such as voting, reading more in the home, and promoting promptness were a few of the suggestions.

I'm afraid that if we don't do some of the things I suggested, we are going to keep seeing them go in and out of jail or dead at an early age. The black community is being devastated by some of the actions of black young men, the school system is struggling mightily to teach these very bright young men; yet, in far too many cases, we are coming up short. Unfortunately, too many of them are not fulfilling the talent they have, nor living up to their potential; so many of them are talented and gifted in so many areas ranging from academics to sports. But, because of their actions and some of the poor choices so many of them are making, these talents go unnoticed. Therefore, they don't benefit from them. Their families don't benefit from them, nor does society. These talents are simply wasted, and used for things that are illegal.

I have a lot of confidence in young black males. If given the right up bringing, a fair number of positive role models, they can do some outstanding things. Many are doing some of these things, such as graduating from high school, staying away from drugs and preparing to have a future.

At the same time, however, far too many are not trying to better their lives. This brief book is about this group and written for parents, teachers, and administrators working with this group. We all have a common interest: wanting desperately for black male youth to improve their chances at being successful.

My objective is to not criticize but to enlighten. There aren't too many occupations out there that afford one the opportunity to impact the world in such a meaningful way than teaching. This profession is unbelievably powerful. The influence we have on children and the impact they have on teachers is quite remarkable.

This relationship also comes with a great deal of responsibility besides just teaching the subject matter. I have a responsibility to my students to teach them to be more than just good students, but also good citizens. That means try hard to always do the right thing, respect yourself, your fellow classmates, your parents, the laws of the land, and play by the rules. Give yourself an opportunity to be successful in life. Don't short change yourself or cheat yourself out of a good life later on by making poor choices early in life.

These are the lessons I teach my students by not simply preaching to them, but modeling these lessons by my actions, by integrating them in my teaching methods, and, yes, by preaching to them sometimes, if it's needed.

In this book, I spoke in direct and plain English about what I think black parents can do to improve the life of their children. I applaud women greatly for their valiant efforts. So many successful men owe their complete success to their mothers. Many were raised solely by their mothers, and unfortunately never knew their fathers. So many women have sacrificed a lot to raise their children. The black community is filled with stories of black women that work two and three jobs to put food on the table, getting only 4 to 5 hours of sleep every night because they spend so much time working. As a teacher, I have seen these situations up close. During my home visits, I've seen the pain on the faces of many mothers when their sons let them down. I've seen the frustration in their eyes because now that the boys are getting so big, she feels powerless, and, therefore, can't control them as easily. I've heard them say, "I will not loose you to the streets," while knowing in her heart that he's already gone. I've heard them say, "I wish your daddy was here." I've heard their cries, while all the while they will never give up on their boys. These women need to be extolled. They need to be recognized and rewarded for their efforts.

My mother was just like these women. She was tough on us, but fair. She had high expectations for my brother and I, and we tried hard to not let her down. We haven't been perfect, but we've worked hard to be successful. My mother was fortunate, and so were my brother and I, because we had a male role model in our house: my father. He worked hard his whole life to give us opportunities that he didn't have. When I was young, I watched him work two and three jobs to provide a quality life for us. For this and all the things he taught us and continues to teach us about life, if I can speak for my brother, we thank him and love him.

Unfortunately, not enough black women and black youth have fathers in the home whose setting the example that so many black male youth need. I'm challenging black men to do better. I understand that there are obstacles. Every black person in America has faced some adversity in some form or another. However, we can't let those obstacles defeat us.

In my years of teaching, I haven't seen many black fathers in the home or come up to the school. I can count the number that I've seen when I was teaching on one hand. I do, however, recall having a conversation with one who came up to the school to talk to me about his son. The lack of confidence the father exhibited was amazing. As he talked to me, he kept his head down. He rarely looked me square in the face. I wasn't sure why. However, I believe he was embarrassed about the fact that he was jobless and having a difficult time making ends meet. He was pretty sure that I knew this, and was therefore embarrassed by it. I tried desperately to put his mind at ease and talked only about his son. The father was supportive and his son was quite productive in school. He studied hard and achieved pretty good grades.

This father was down on himself, but he was determined to improve his life. I'm not sure if he ever did, but his son respected him a great deal, notwithstanding his economic misfortunes. I think other fathers can learn a valuable lesson from him. You don't have to have a great deal of money to influence your children in positive ways. Being there with them, and teaching them about life, is what they will remember most. Often times, I hear other black men say, "I wish I could do more for my kids." Or, "I want my child to have the best." Indeed, those are plausible things to say. I'm sure the kids feel the same way. However, they cherish the time you spend with them more than your ability to buy them material things.

I want black men to recognize this. I want them to understand that their sons need them more today than anytime before. With so many negative influences out there, black boys will face many challenges and encounter many obstacles. With the help of their fathers, they can overcome them. Fathers have to be there to give advice, model good behavior, and reward their sons when they do well. They have to be there to encourage their sons, when adversities come, and teach them to not give up. Fathers have to educate their sons on the limitless opportunities that exist in life, if they make good decisions.

The education that fathers can provide will prepare their sons to be good fathers and hopefully this will continue for future generations. In so many homes, there's a cycle of fathers and sons going in and out of jail, a cycle of fathers abandoning their sons, a cycle of fathers and sons not utilizing the capabilities that they have. Indeed, this cycle is hard to break because the proper role models are not around, or there are not enough of them.

That doesn't mean, however, that the cycle can't be broken. In many families it's being broken everyday. Many black young men I talk to that are successful didn't have fathers around when they were growing up. They did not let that discourage them. They worked hard in school to make something out of themselves.

Unfortunately, however, far too many black youth aren't able to overcome the lack of fathers in the home. They aren't able to overcome the challenges that female single-headed homes face. They don't have that person there who they identify with physically or maybe even mentally, in some cases, to help shape their development. Therefore, growing up is difficult. It's even challenging with both parents around. However, without the help of both parents it's especially difficult.

The psychological impact that fatherless homes have on the mind set of black boys is devastating. The feelings of abandonment, powerlessness, and insecurity have been illustrated by many of the boys I have taught. Although I'm not a psychologist, I'm speaking from what I have witnessed and experienced. More times than not, I can identify students that have fathers in their lives and those that don't or have very limited access to their fathers. Those that don't or have limited access seem to respond to authority figures less favorably. Why they do is something that can be studied, debated, and researched for years. This book is being written to inform fathers that their sons need them now and to equip those that teach black males with the proper tools to better relate to them.

Indeed, many show that they need their fathers in their lives and are crying out for their help by being mischievous in school, in an effort to get their father's attention, and by showing a disregard for authority figures because they are angry for not having a relationship with their fathers.

Unfortunately, when the youth grow up, the cries are louder and more destructive. Joining gangs, quitting school, and doing even illegal things are some of the cries that take place. It's clear that not enough people in the lives of these youth are listening to their cries or perhaps they don't know how to respond to them. Nevertheless the end results are the same: Black males continue to be overrepresented in penal institutions, be overrepresented in alternative schools and continue to show a dislike for school.

Indeed, black male youth are no different than anyone else. It's just that the environment in which many of them grow up in is different. This can be changed if fathers take a more active role. I hope fathers that read this book understand why I'm pleading with them to build strong relationships with their sons and give them the tools necessary to be successful. These tools consist of three things: self-confidence, self-respect, and self-worth.

All center on the word self. Not enough black male youth truly know themselves and what they are capable of, largely because in too many cases fathers aren't there to show them who they are, how to be productive in society, and how to overcome adversity in route to becoming successful.

In short, black fathers it's time to get more focused. We have a job to do, a job that is more important than the one we go to everyday. Many of us can do better at doing this job. Those that are already doing it, your sons appreciate it, and so does society. However, for those that feel they aren't doing the best they can, try harder. Commit to doing better. If we don't take this challenge, our sons will miss out on a great deal and so will future generations.

Notes

1. Chicago Tribune (May, 2004) Bill Cosby
2. Hanson, Mark E. (1996) Educational Administration and Organizational Behavior. (Allyn and Bacon Needham Heights, Massachusetts).
3. Thurow, Lester. (1992). Head to Head: The Coming Economics Battle among Japan, Europe and America. (William Morrow and Company Inc. New York).
4. Twentieth Century Task Force on Employment Problems of Black Youth. (1971). The Job Crisis for Black Youth Report. New York, Praeger.
5. U.S. Department of Education, National Center for Education Statistics, Dropout Rates in the United States (2001).

Made in the USA